# L.A. BIKE RIDES

# L.A. BIKE RIDES

A Guide to 37 Specially Selected Bicycle
Routes in Los Angeles County

**Loren MacArthur**

CHRONICLE BOOKS • SAN FRANCISCO

Editor: Catherine Pearsall
Composition: Words & Windows
Book and cover design: Diana Fairbanks
Cover photography: Mark Aronoff
   (Scene from Ride 22)

Library of Congress Cataloging in
Publication Data

Mac Arthur, Loren.
L.A. bike rides.

Includes index.
1. Bicycle touring—California—
Los Angeles County—Guide-books.
2. Bicycle touring—California—
3. Los Angeles County (Calif.)—
Description and travel—Guide-books.
I. Title.
II. Title: LA bike rides.
GV1045.5.C22L676   1985
917.94′93   85-7865
ISBN 0-87701-316-0 (pbk.)

Chronicle Books
One Hallidie Plaza
San Francisco, CA 94102

*This book is dedicated
to Heidi Yorkshire*

# CONTENTS

# ACKNOWLEDGMENTS

I want to thank the friends and strangers who made writing this book easier:

Lloyd Beauchain (now retired) and Eugene Gagne of the Los Angeles County Flood Control District, whose encyclopedic knowledge of local water history and current flood control operations aided me immensely; Sara Hamel and Rick Gordon, who each supplied me with copious notes on bike rides they have done; Father Molaise Meehan of St. Andrew's Priory, who introduced me to bicycling in the high desert; Sierra Club leaders Art Rich, for his enthusiastic discussion of bicycling safety, and Ron Webster, for his many insights on bicycle trails and knowledge of wildlife; and Carl Golomb, City of Pico Rivera, whose knowledge of bicycle trail planning enriched my background knowledge.

A number of city, state, and agency employees not only gave freely and cheerfully of their time and knowledge but did far more than requested to help out: Gail L. Wasil, Tidelands Agency; Henry Fuhrmann, Jet Propulsion Laboratory; Kathy Phillips, City of Arcadia; Mrs. Sally Colby, librarian for the Californiana Collection at the Rosemead Branch of the Los Angeles County Library; Alan Jones, State of California Department of Water Resources; William Naylor, City of Montebello; Sally Erickson, Southwest Museum; Lu Ann Munns, Los Angeles County Arboretum; and John Estrada, American Youth Hostel.

A special note of thanks goes to friends in the Mensa Bicycling Special Interest Group, with whom I first rode out on the bicycle trails in Los Angeles. My mother's unwavering belief in me gave me the self confidence to tackle a job like writing. For that, I am forever grateful to Adele Mac Arthur.

Finally, and especially, my love and thanks to Tom Kearney, whose support and encouragement speeded the completion of this book, and to Duncan Bock, who sat and observed everything, commenting when necessary.

# INTRODUCTION

In the fall of 1983 I set out to ride all of the bicycle trails in Los Angeles County. I decided to find these trails one Sunday as I attempted to pedal my way through a crush of bicycles, tandems, go-carts, roller skaters, pedestrians and dogs, all on the South Bay Bicycle Trail in Venice. Like most of the weekend bikers there, I didn't know where else to bike; and when I went to buy a guide, I couldn't find one.

*L.A. Bike Rides* tells you where else you can go after you've ridden the South Bay Bicycle Trail. It is the result of more than 1,200 miles of bicycle riding that took me north, south, east, and west in Los Angeles County to search out and explore the bike trails described here.

Los Angeles has more off-road bicycle trails than any other urban county in the United States. More than 200 miles of bike paths follow our waterways: the rivers, creeks, dry washes, aqueducts, reservoirs, lakes, and ocean. Most of these trails are unknown to all but a few bicycle riders and rarely used. They range in length from .8 mile to 107 miles and offer endless opportunities for safe, scenic, freewheeling bicycle trips. *L.A. Bike Rides* tells bikers how to find and use these trails.

Cyclists who follow these bikeways will discover a different Los Angeles, full of hidden beauty and unexpected delights. Along the California Aqueduct a magnificent blue heron soared in front of me; and later a coyote stopped to stare at me with his wild, yellow eyes. In the San Gabriel Valley after the rains, great sheets of water poured over the holding dams along the San Gabriel River, creating sparkling waterfalls.

Although the South Bay Bicycle Trail is crowded, its status as Los Angeles' most popular bike trail is deserved: it passes through some of the most spectacular scenery you can find in Southern California. And, although we know our freeways intimately from riding on them so much, the bicycle trails offer a final new perspective. The trails pass under almost every freeway in the county: it is like taking a tunnel to a futuristic, subsurface colony.

There is a paradox in riding a car 20 miles to take a 15-mile bike ride; but we are, after all, Angelenos, and should be able to live with it. Portable bicycle racks costing around $20 fit on the backs of most cars. The racks take about three minutes to fasten in place. Available in bicycle shops, they carry two or three bicycles and make driving with one's bike an easy task.

I should mention that I began my explorations for the book with some trepidation. Would the gangs who reputedly occupy the parks in various areas harass me? As a woman, would I be safe? I did more than half of my riding alone and encountered nothing but friendliness, questions and good will. I did come across many groups of boys. Their favorite congregating places included the tops of the graded cement pylons that support the freeway underpasses. They were very busy just sitting around, and the question they asked the most often was, "What time is it?" In more than a year the biggest "incident" occurred when I smiled and waved at a group of teenagers near the Whittier Narrows Dam, and one had temerity to shout back, "Hey, Granny!" I considered turning back and explaining I was probably younger than his mother, but it seemed beneath my dignity.

I began my explorations sober and reserved and a bit worried about my reception in the many areas where I didn't speak the language. I soon learned that a smile and a wave brought responses of a warmth and friendliness I had never expected. (Following directions given in a foreign language, however, is very difficult.) I hope your experience on these bike trails reaps even greater rewards.

## How To Use This Book

The headings at the beginning of each trip description are designed to help you choose the right ride for you and your group. Here is an explanation of the headings:

**Distance:** The distance listed is the round trip mileage. Families with small children and out-of-shape adults should begin with rides 10 miles or under. A few weekends of biking will soon condition you for the 20 to 30 mile rides.

**General Location:** This heading gives the area where the ride is located.

**Features:** Highlights of the ride are described, and any special conditions are noted.

**Difficulty:** The rides are rated Easy, Moderate and Strenuous, taking into account hills, condition of the path and length of the ride.

An Easy ride will be fairly level and around 10 miles round trip—or less. There will almost certainly be underpasses to negotiate. Beginners may need to walk up an occasional grade.

A Moderate ride is about 15 to 20 miles round trip and usually has one or more grades to climb—the face of a dam or a seaside bluff, for example.

A Difficult ride may be short or long, but it will have substantial grades to climb and should only be attempted by conditioned bikers.

All judgments of difficulty are subjective, and bikers who are not sure of their abilities may wish to begin with an easy ride, see how they feel after completing the ride, and use the experience as a basis for comparing other trips in the book.

**Getting There:** This heading gives explicit instructions for driving to the ride from the nearest freeways and, once there, for finding parking, both paid and free.

**Finding the Trail:** The location of the trailhead and how to ride to it from the parking area are explained.

**Description:** Points of interest along the way and any confusing turns or detours are described in this section. Total distance from the trailhead in tenths of miles is given in parentheses at street undercrossings (0.6), trail junctions (1.7), and so forth.

**Linking:** This special section tells bikers how to extend their rides by linking up to nearby trails.

## Safety

It is paradoxical that off-road bike trails, built to be safe, are avoided by experienced bikers, who consider them more dangerous than city streets. Although I have ridden all the Los Angeles bike trails—many of them several times—with no accidents and not even any close calls, I have seen numerous potentially dangerous situations. The danger comes from inexperience: casual bikers who don't know the safety rules and a public who is unused to bicyclists and bicycle trails and unsure of how to deal with them.

Staying safe means knowing the accepted (although unwritten) rules of biking and following them.

**Stopping and Starting:** Riding along, listening to the wind and the water, you can easily forget that your bicycle is noiseless, as is the one behind you. A sudden stop may make it impossible for the rider behind you to avoid a crash. *Always* check behind you and pull to the side of the path before stopping. When starting up again, look behind you for approaching riders before moving onto the bike path.

**Passing:** Again, remember your bicycle is silent. Cyclists, roller skaters and pedestrians in front of you will not know you are there wanting to pass unless you tell them so. The standard phrase used by bikers who wish to pass is, "On your left." This statement is uttered in agreeable tones soon enough to allow those ahead to react, preferably by moving right. The biker then passes on the left. Since this standardized phrase is unknown to non-bikers, a friendly "Passing" often gets better results.

**Pedestrians and Other Unexpected Obstacles:** Always watch for pedestrians who cross the bike path without first checking for bicyclists. Most near collisions I have observed occurred because fast-moving bikers had to slam on the brakes to avoid hitting a pedestrian or another biker. Cyclists who like to ride fast are best off avoiding the popular bikeways, which are used more for a social event than a biking experience.

Following these simple rules about starting, stopping and passing will eliminate most dangers on Los Angeles' few crowded bike trails. Nearly all the trails described in this book are so unused it is rare to pass a group of bikers, much less run into them.

**Helmets:** Many bikers ride these paths without wearing a helmet. Ever since reading how a head can split open like a ripe tomato as it hits the pavement after a bicycle accident, I have personally worn a helmet. Bareheaded bikers should be aware that the potential seriousness of any accident increases geometrically when the head is unprotected.

**Street Intersections:** More than 95 percent of bicycle accidents occur at intersections. Although few rides in this book cross city streets, those that do usually cross them in the middle of the block, creating a potentially dangerous situation. Accidents occur because automobile drivers do not expect bicycle riders, do not look for them and thus do not see them. Wearing bright clothes helps the biker's visibility, but the safest way to cross a mid-block intersection is to ride to a corner with a light, dismount the bike and walk across, wheeling the bike. Street crossings will be listed for each ride in the book.

**Street Routes:** Marked bike routes along city streets require special precautions. Bikers must stay alert for drivers opening their car doors into the bike route. Cars making a right in front of you without signaling are a particular hazard. Watch for them and for cars leaving driveways and parking lots. Again, the few rides with segments along city streets will be listed.

**Common Sense:** It is unpleasant to travel without a water bottle. About half the water faucets I found along these rides were broken. Some had been repaired when I returned to ride a second time. Do not expect water faucets mentioned in ride descriptions to work. When water does pour out of one of them, it will be a pleasant surprise.

It is equally unpleasant to get a flat tire on a deserted bike trail and have no way to repair it. Always carry a small tool kit that includes a set of tire irons, a patch kit (or a spare tube), pump, wrench, and screwdriver. Two portable, basic repair manuals that I can recommend with confidence are *The Bike Bag Book* by Tom Cuthbertson (Berkeley: Ten Speed Press, 1981; $2.95) and the

*Xyzyx Bicycle Repair* series (Canoga Park: Xyzyx Information Corp., 1972; $4.95) with editions for coasters and three speeds as well as ten-speed bicycles. When the *Xyzyx* series tells you how to change a tire, it starts with a picture of a wheel with an arrow pointing to it and a caption reading Wheel. It is difficult to go wrong with instructions like these, even if you don't know the difference between a hex key and an Allen wrench. Cuthbertson's book, a condensation of his *Anybody's Bike Book*, is written specifically for emergency roadside bicycle repair. Four by 6½ inches, it weighs only 2 ounces and covers all common breakdown problems.

Bicycle theft appears to be the greatest hazard encountered by Angeleno bikers. Park rangers throughout the county warned me to always lock my bicycle if I planned to leave it. I carry a lock and chain that weigh two pounds and still wonder if I will find my bike where I left it. I am reminded of the annual Iowa RAGBRAI—the 500-mile, trans-Iowa bike ride that attracts 8,000 riders each year. We Californians arrived in Iowa for the 1981 ride weighted with massive chains and impregnable locks. We quickly learned we could drop our bikes anywhere, leave them unguarded and unlocked, and return to find them and the contents of our bike bags untouched. We may have lost our innocence and honesty in Los Angeles, but we still have some of the world's best bike rides. I hope you enjoy them as I have.

## For More Information

Free maps of many of the bicycle routes described in *L.A. Bike Rides* are available from city and county offices.

CALTRANS District 7 offers an excellent packet including maps of the California Aqueduct Bikeway, the South Bay Bicycle Trail and the river trails; the packet also contains information on commuter bicycling, Park 'n' Ride lots with bicycle lockers, and laws concerning bicyclists. Write:

State of California
Department of Transportation
P.O. Box 2304, Terminal Annex
Los Angeles, California 90051
Telephone: (213) 620-3550 (Public Information)

The Los Angeles City Department of Transportation sends the most complete set of information. Besides the CALTRANS packet described above, it also mails a map of the Los Angeles County major off-road bike routes and excellent maps of individual bike paths in the city of Los Angeles. Write:

Department of Transportation
City of Los Angeles
Room 1200, City Hall
Los Angeles, California 90012
Telephone: (213) 485-3051

The city of Arcadia sends a map of its bike routes. Write:

Recreation Department
240 West Huntington Drive
Arcadia, California 91006
Telephone: (818) 405-4191

The city of Pasadena sends a map of the Kenneth Newell Bikeway and of bike lanes and bike routes within the city. Write:

Public Works Department
Room 211, City Hall
100 N. Garfield Avenue
Pasadena, California 91109
Telephone: (818) 405-4191

A pamphlet published by the Automobile Club of Southern California lists general information about 51 bike trails (maps of the trails are not given) in Southern California, including 18 bike trails and routes in Los Angeles County. The booklet is available to members only.

A number of books on bicycling and bicycle maintenance are available. Local bicycle stores usually carry a good selection.

Although *Bike Touring* (San Francisco: Sierra Club Books, 1979; $7.95), the Sierra Club guide by Raymond Bridge, is aimed at bikers who go on overnight tours, it has excellent general information on choosing a bicycle, equipment, repair tools, and clothing as well as chapters on learning to ride and bicycle safety.

Besides the repair manuals mentioned earlier, Tom Cuthbertson's *Anybody's Bike Book* (Berkeley: Ten Speed Press, 1979; $4.95), on bicycle repairs gives clear, detailed instructions comprehensible to beginning mechanics. The book is intended for home rather than on-trail use.

The University of California Press publishes a series of nature guides that are excellent for carrying along on a bike ride because they are lightweight and compact. Titles of interest to Angelenos include: *Native Trees of Southern California, Cacti of California, Native Shrubs of Southern California, Early Uses of California Plants,* and *Introduction to the Natural History of Southern California.*

# I The River Trails

*The streams that run off in places follow narrow canyons or gorges down their sides, and as soon as they strike the plain or valley spread out wide and generally sink. These "washes" or dry beds are often two or three miles wide, covered with bowlders and sand, supporting only a vegetation or stunted shrubs, from five to ten feet high . . .*

—WILLIAM H. BREWER
Up and Down California in 1860–1864

Some of Los Angeles' best and longest bicycle trails run along the levees built to contain our three biggest rivers, the Los Angeles, the Rio Hondo, and the San Gabriel. Angelenos owe these trails to the devastating floods that perenially destroy sections of Los Angeles. In 1915, to control the flooding, the county formed the Los Angeles Flood Control District. Through the years, the district has built one of the largest flood control systems in the history of engineering.

Today a 90 mile system of connecting bikeways follows the levees that have cemented down our once wild rivers. The scenery along these river trails changes drastically by season. After the rains, the uncemented sections of the rivers flow full, sending dancing waterfalls over holding dams and flooding the bottomlands with sparkling lakes. During the dry season the water disappears; dry washes of cracked mud and gritty sand lined with drooping, dusty bushes are the only indication that water ran here just a few months ago. Bikers are advised to ride these trails after the rains, when the rivers are full and the air is clean.

The river rides are:

**Ride 1.** West Fork Bike Trail. A moderate ride in the San Gabriel Mountains following a level service road beside the West Fork of the San Gabriel River.

**Rides 2, 3, 4, 5, and 6.** San Gabriel River Bike Trail. Easy and moderate rides along 38 miles of the San Gabriel from the mountains to the sea.

**Rides 7 and 8.** Upper Rio Hondo Bike Trail. Easy rides along the Rio Hondo on little-used trails.

**Rides 9 and 10.** Lario Trail. Two rides along the Rio Hondo and Los Angeles River to the Pacific Ocean.

**Ride 11.** Los Angeles River Bike Trail. A short ride along an unknown and badly maintained bicycle trail.

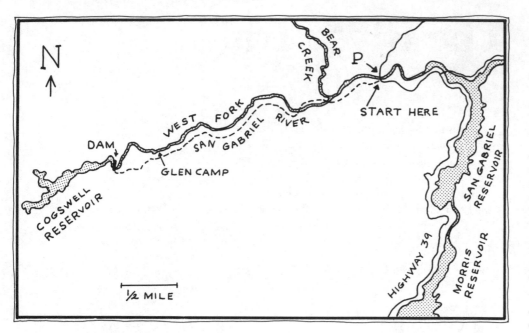

## RIDE 1

# West Fork Bike Trail

**Distance:** 12.4 miles round trip to Glen campground; 14.4 miles round trip to Cogswell Reservoir

**General Location:** Angeles National Forest

**Features:** This trail winds through a scenic river canyon in the local mountains beside the West Fork of the San Gabriel River; yet unlike almost every other mountain road, it has no ups and downs: it is a comparatively level ride with a barely perceptible elevation gain on a service road closed to public traffic.

The forested canyon and abundant seasonal wild flowers make this ride one of the prettiest in the book. The river, fed from Cogswell Reservoir at the end of the ride and from Bear Creek to the north, runs all year and provides several fairly sheltered swimming holes. It is a favorite spot for fisher people. The canyon floor is at an elevation of 2,000 feet, and cyclists should remember their breath will be shorter than at sea level.

Two variations are suggested for this ride; the first stops at Glen Camp. The longer ride includes the steepest hill in this book and goes all the way to the bridge at Cogswell Dam. Occasional snows fall on the road but melt quickly. The ride may be taken at any time of year except immediately after heavy rains when side streams flowing over the road make it dangerous.

**Difficulty:** Moderate, Glen Camp loop. Strenuous, Cogswell Dam loop.

The pleasures of this ride are not only in seeing the lush trees and gurgling stream along the way but in tackling a road that is in places bumpy, rutted, gravelly, or slippery. From experience we assume our bike trails will be groomed: smooth and free of debris. On the West Fork you know you're riding on Mother Earth because she intrudes so often upon the pavement. Rutted sections are intermingled with several smooth stretches of pavement where the road was most recently rebuilt after flash floods tore it out (the road is intermittently washed out by storm runoff). One final note: the canyon chills quickly in the afternoon when the sun leaves; carry a sweater.

**Elevation Gain:** 440 feet, trail head to Glen Camp; 840 feet, trail head to Cogswell Dam

**Getting There:** Exit the Foothill Freeway (I-210) north on Azusa Avenue (Highway 39). Drive north 8.7 miles past Morris Reservoir to the north end of San Gabriel Reservoir. Stay left at the road intersection and continue 1.6 miles to the bridge crossing the West Fork of the San Gabriel. Park in the free lot at the north end of the bridge on the west side of the highway.

**Finding the Trail:** Ride back across the bridge. The trail leaves from Highway 39 on the south bank of the river. The service road is blocked with a locked gate. Bikers should lift bikes over the low barrier across the narrow bike entrance. (These barriers, about 1 foot high, are intended to keep out motorcycles and other motorized vehicles. They will be referred to as entrance barriers throughout the book.)

**Description:** The melody of water rushing over the boulder filled river bed welcomes bikers as they start up the trail. The West Fork is a popular gathering place for fisher people and strollers with whom bikers will share the road for the first half mile. Casual visitors soon disappear, however, leaving the road wide open for cyclists.

The trail is marked by mileposts on the road's north shoulder, although several of them have disappeared; the remaining posts tell bikers how far they have ridden. Bear Creek enters the West Fork at .9 mile (a hiking trail crosses the river and heads up the creek), and at 1 mile the road crosses the river at the first bridge and follows the north bank for the next half mile.

A second bridge at 1.6 miles returns the road to the south bank. The river is closed to fishing from the second bridge upstream. The reason for this closure is an interesting story of the conflicting uses of Southern California's water resources. Cogswell Dam was built on the West Fork by the Los Angeles County Flood Control District for the primary purpose of flood control. Before the dam was built, the river dried up in summer; but with the dam's controlled release of water, the West Fork became a year-round river and a popular recreational area managed by the U.S. Forest Service, owner of the land on either side of the river. The river became known for its trout fishing.

However, by 1981 heavy silt had built up behind the dam, and the flood control district decided to sluice the silt down the river. Instead of the 4,000 cubic yards of silt that was expected in the runoff, 60,000 cubic yards of silt poured out of the dam, creating a river of mud that flowed down the canyon destroying animal life in the river as it went. The river lost its ability to maintain insect life on which fish live. The fishing closure above the second bridge is an attempt to reestablish the river as a natural stream by leaving it alone. It is an irony to ponder: the dam, which created the year-round home for fish, also destroyed it.

Several waterfalls (also intermittent) cascade down the south bank, providing a refreshing pause for bikers. A large waterfall appears at 2.8 miles; and following a gain in elevation at 3.4 miles, bikers will arrive at a pleasant gravelly beach (4.2). The river runs through a series of rapids here, and provides interesting scenery for a rest stop. A second beach is located at 5.1 miles, and Glen Camp soon appears (6.2). The camp has picnic tables, garbage cans and pit toilets. Situated on a low bluff above the river, it offers nice views and an excellent place to picnic.

Bikers on the shorter ride should return to the highway from Glen Camp. Those continuing to the dam now begin a 1 mile uphill ride that includes a 240 foot gain in .4 mile. Many bikers walk it, unashamed. At 7 miles a fence with an open gate crosses the road. Posted signs warn that trespassing is forbidden. However, bikers have permission to stay on the road to the dam. This privilege exists only at the goodwill of the flood control district, and bikers are expected to stay off the property around the dam operator's home. Violations of this request will close the road down to everyone.

Views from the dam (7.2) down the canyon to the east make the ride up worth the effort. The return ride from the dam to Glen Camp should be taken carefully. The road is steep, rutted and gravelly, with several sharp turns.

# SAN GABRIEL RIVER TRAIL

The San Gabriel River as we know it today exists only because tenants of Don Pio Pico, California's last Mexican governor, built a ditch at the wrong time in the wrong place. In 1867 the San Gabriel flowed through the Whittier Narrows and disappeared into the Los Angeles River nine miles away. That winter the largest flood the San Gabriel Valley had known in years swept down the river, found the irrigation ditch dug by Pico's tenants, and jumped its bed to flow along the ditch and cut a new channel to the Pacific Ocean. The new river ran parallel to the Los Angeles River, only six miles east of it.

Residents called it New River. After deciding it was there to stay, they named it the San Gabriel River and renamed the old San Gabriel the Rio Hondo—or Deep River.

Riding down the cement levees of these rivers in their current emasculated state, it is difficult to imagine the destruction they caused, or where all the water came from. In our semi-arid landscape, it is interesting to note that, in 1926, .65 inch of rain fell in one minute at Opid's Camp near the head-

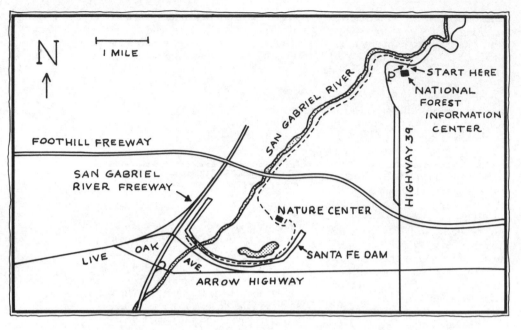

## RIDE 2

SAN GABRIEL RIVER TRAIL

# San Gabriel Mountains to Santa Fe Dam

**Distance:** 10.4 miles round trip to Santa Fe Dam Recreation Area; 15.2 miles round trip to Santa Fe Dam outlet

**General Location:** Azusa, Irwindale

**Features:** Following the San Gabriel River as it leaves the San Gabriel Mountains, this trail provides sweeping views of the mountains and the wild, semiarid landscape of the undeveloped river bottomland. Entering the Santa Fe Dam Recreation Area, bikers ride through an exotic natural cactus garden where two signed nature paths provide an opportunity for detailed study of the area's ecology. In the developed area of the park, a large lake is used for boating and swimming. Riding along the top of the dam, which is 4.5 miles long, cyclists have splendid views of the extensive bottomland and park below.

**Difficulty:** Easy, Santa Fe Dam Recreation Area. Moderate, Santa Fe Dam outlet.

**Getting There:** Exit the Foothill Freeway (I-210) north on Azusa Avenue (Highway 39). Drive north to the junction of Azusa Avenue and San Gabriel Canyon Road. Continue north on San Gabriel Canyon Road .8 mile to the National Forest Information Center on the right. Park in the free lot there.

waters of the San Gabriel River. For many years that statistic held as the nation's record for a minute's rainfall.

Although approximately 10 miles of the San Gabriel channel have been cemented, almost 30 miles run free. It is an exhilarating experience to ride this New River (it celebrated its 100th birthday only in 1968) from the mountains to the sea. Here are the rides along the trail:

**Ride 2.** San Gabriel Mountains to Santa Fe Dam. A moderate ride along the winding gravel beds of the San Gabriel to the Santa Fe Dam.

**Ride 3.** Santa Fe Dam to Legg Lake. A 19 mile round trip ride from the dam to the bottomland of the Whitter Narrows.

**Ride 4.** Whittier Narrows Dam to Wilderness Park. From this overgrown bottomland of the Narrows to a cheerful park, this ride offers an optional stop at the Pio Pico hacienda.

**Ride 5.** Wilderness Park to El Dorado Park. This trip follows the river 16.8 miles round trip to the lakes and nature trail in El Dorado Park.

**Ride 6.** El Dorado Park to the Pacific Ocean. This easy ride concludes the San Gabriel River Trail by following the river 20.8 miles round trip to its outlet into the Pacific at the Long Beach Marina.

**Finding the Trail:** The bike trail begins on the west side of San Gabriel Canyon Road opposite to and slightly north of the ranger station.

**Description:** The raised trail allows sweeping views of the exposed rock beds and multi-channels of the San Gabriel River. For millions of years this area was subject to periodic flooding during the winter rains. The torrential waters carried boulders, small rocks, and sand to the valley floor; in some places the bed of rock and gravel is more than 100 feet thick. The bike trail passes through the center of this broad alluvial plain; towering gravel plants dot the area.

The stillness created by this vast, rocky desert is shattered farther on as the trail passes the San Gabriel Valley Gun Club in the hills beyond the river. Situated so the canyon provides a natural echoing board, the gun club sounds like a perpetual Fourth of July fireworks display.

At 2.4 miles the trail passes the Santa Fe Equestrian Staging Area, which provides an entrance to the horse trail paralleling the bike path. Water and rest rooms are available at the staging area. A Bike Trail sign here indicates the direction to the Whittier Narrows; bikers should follow it. The path crosses under Foothill Boulevard (3.0) and takes a sharp curve under Foothill Freeway (3.1) just east of its intersection with the San Gabriel River Freeway. As bikers ride beside the river, they can see the results of the violent action of the river in flood. Residue left by flooding surrounds the spillway where the river passes under the freeway. Great washes of boulders lie on banks cut in a succession of shoulders by the torrential waters.

One of the delights of this trail comes into view as bikers enter the Santa Fe Dam Nature Area: a natural cactus garden. Odd-shaped valley cholla, yucca and prickly pear grow alongside the Mormon tea bush. The yucca is the most spectacular of these plants. It lives 12 years; during its last year it sends up a tall stalk that grows six inches a day and flowers within two weeks. The Indians used its fibrous leaves for baskets, ate its roasted stalk and berries, and made shampoo from its roots.

The nature area is a 1,000 acre preserve set aside to protect the last vestiges of the flood basin vegetative community from development. At 4.2 miles a Trail Sign points riders north around the park headquarters, which also serves as the nature center. Several interesting display boards tell the history of the area and show the native plants growing in the area. Two nature trails leave from the center. The shorter trail is a 15 minute stroll; the longer trail provides a more detailed look at the local flora. Bike racks, water, rest rooms and benches make the center a pleasant rest stop.

The bike trail runs east from park headquarters, then turns sharply south (4.6) to circumvent the nature preserve.

The trail soon arrives at the Santa Fe Dam Recreation Area (5.2), an extensive, grassy park with a 70 acre lake that is the focus of activity. Lifeguards are on duty at a roped-off swimming area which protects swimmers from the boaters. Boats are for rent at $5 an hour, and during the summer YWCA and private sailing lessons are offered. There are pony rides for children and escorted horseback rides for adults. Group hayrides are available at $75 an hour; for information and reservations, call (818) 969-6615. Paths (not specifically for bicycles) follow the lake shore,

and viewing platforms provide pleasant rest stops. Refreshments, rest rooms, bike racks and water are available at the park, which is open 10 to 5 all year.

Bikers taking the longer ride should follow the Bike Trail sign up the road to the top of the dam's east end (5.3). The park entrance is on top of the dam. At the entrance kiosk, the trail swings east for an exhilarating 2-mile ride along the crest of the dam. Halfway across the dam, the trail makes a swift descent down the west face of the dam. Turning sharply east, it runs between two chain link fences before arriving at the outlet (7.6). When the river is running, the outlet becomes a contemporary water sculpture: a great curving arc of cement with a fast-flowing sheet of water coursing over it.

The dam, completed in 1949, was built for flood control. The reservoir area behind the dam is 1,088 acres; it drains 236 square miles and can hold 34,300 acre feet of water. Elevation at the top of the dam is 513 feet; the bike path drops 58 feet to the outlet.

**Linking:** An additional 16.8 mile round trip loop continuing south on the San Gabriel Trail leads to the Whittier Narrows Recreation Area, where bikers may visit Legg Lake or ride to the top of Whittier Dam. *See Ride 3* for details.

This ride ends at the dam outlet. The return trip is by the same trail in reverse.

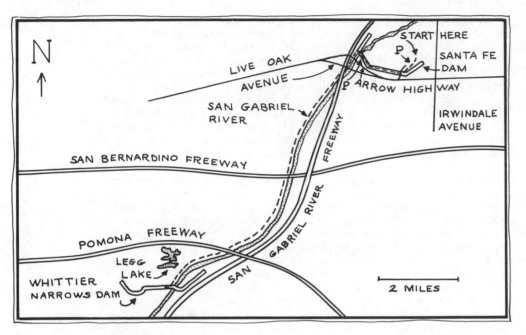

## RIDE 3

SAN GABRIEL RIVER TRAIL

# Santa Fe Dam to Legg Lake

**Distance:** 19 miles round trip from Santa Fe Dam outlet; 24.2 miles round trip from Santa Fe Dam Recreation Area

**General Location:** Irwindale, Arcadia, El Monte, and South El Monte

**Features:** Leaving the monolithic structure of Santa Fe Dam, this trail follows the San Gabriel River to the bottomland of the Whittier Narrows. The Whittier Narrows Dam, which contains the floodwaters of both the Rio Hondo and

San Gabriel, is the final massive dam in the extensive Los Angeles flood control project. The trail runs beside the Whittier Narrows Wildlife Sanctuary, a verdant, lush wilderness where cyclists may expect to see rabbits bounding across the bike trail. Groves of sycamores and willows grow beside Legg Lake, which is encircled by a bike path. Side trips may be taken to the top of the dam, the Whittier Narrows Recreation Area visitors center, and the nature center.

**Difficulty:** Moderate

**Getting There:** From the San Gabriel River Freeway (I-605), exit east on Live Oak Avenue and drive 1 mile to its

junction with Arrow Highway. Continue east on Arrow Highway 2 miles. Turn left into the entrance to the Santa Fe Recreation Area, which is open 10 to 5 daily. Fees: $2 automobile, $4 recreation vehicle, 20 feet or longer, $1 senior citizens.

For free parking drive east on Live Oak Avenue past its junction with Arrow Highway. Make a U-turn and drive northwest on Arrow Highway to the dam outlet. The parking area there is free. (There is no left turn from Live Oak to Arrow, which necessitates a U-turn.)

From the Foothill Freeway (I-210), exit south on Irwindale Avenue and drive 1.5 miles to Arrow Highway. Turn west on Arrow, then north into the Santa Fe Dam Recreation Area parking. For free parking, continue west on Arrow to the dam outlet.

**Finding the Trail:** From the recreation area, ride to the top of the dam on the same road used to enter the park. At the entrance kiosk, swing west and ride 2 miles along the crest of the dam. Just past the halfway point, the trail makes a swift descent down the west face of the dam to the outlet. Trip mileage will be given starting at the dam outlet. From the dam outlet, cross to the south side of Arrow Highway. The trail begins on the west bank of the San Gabriel River. Beginning the ride in the recreation area adds 5.2 miles round trip to the distance.

**Description:** The San Gabriel River, which has been bottled up behind the dam, is a dry wash at the start of the ride. The river bed drops almost imperceptibly to the Whittier Dam; beside it, the bike trail descends in a series of steps separated by long, level shoulders.

Sweeping views of the San Bernardino Mountains to the north and the wide river channel with clumps of willows along its banks to the south dominate the scenery. East of the path several old and deep gravel quarries are gradually filling with water; one of them is easily viewed from the bike path (1.8).

The Ramona Boulevard Rest Area is west of the path down a steep path to the foot of the levee directly after crossing under Ramona Boulevard (3.2). A pipe sticking out of the ground is actually a water faucet. A small lever on one side of the pipe shoots out a stream of water. A second, similar rest stop is located at Valley Boulevard (4.7).

The apparently dry river has suddenly begun to fill with water which would appear to come from underground springs. However, cyclists who look carefully just before arriving at Valley Boulevard will see Walnut Creek flowing into the San Gabriel from the east. At about 5.5 miles the river has become a teeming bird sanctuary. Bird songs drown out the noise of the nearby San Gabriel River Freeway. Snowy egrets—beautiful long-legged birds—are among the many species that frequent the river here.

A small rodeo ring has been built beside the levee at 6.2 miles, and bikers have balcony seats to view the local competitions frequently held there on weekends. On one trip we watched a roping contest where the small calves let out of the chute wore plastic horns over their real horns. The plastic horns, intended as a safety measure, were tied under the calves' chins like spring Easter bonnets. (No one, by the way, managed to rope one of the bounding beasts.)

After crossing under the Pomona Freeway (6.8) and Peck Road (7.1), the trail passes through the most beautiful section of the ride; the path here runs beside the Whittier Narrows Wildlife Sanctuary. The sanctuary was set aside to preserve some of the river bottomland in its natural state; thickets of lush, tangled growth provide a sheltering home for rabbits, raccoons and skunks.

The trail soon arrives at the Four Point Trail Intersection (8.4), where bikers may continue directly to Legg Lake or take several side trips.

Linking: The Whittier Narrows Dam looms up directly south of the intersection. Fine views of the bottomland may be had by riding up the back of the dam and west along its crest to Rosemead Boulevard (2.4 miles round trip).

A second Trail Sign at the intersection points to the Rio Hondo Trail. This trail leads to the intersection of Rosemead Boulevard and Durfee Avenue. To reach the Rio Hondo Trail, cross to the northeast corner of Rosemead and ride west on San Gabriel Boulevard (Durfee becomes San Gabriel here). To ride north on the Rio Hondo Trail, turn east at the Bike Trail sign before crossing the bridge over the Rio Hondo. *See Ride 8.* To ride south to the Lario Trail, cross the bridge and turn south across San Gabriel at the Bike Trail sign located at the street light at Lincoln Boulevard. *See Ride 9.*

A third alternative at the Four Point intersection is to continue south on the San Gabriel River Trail. Ride up the dam, then follow the trail south down the face of the dam. *See Ride 4.*

The Legg Lake ride follows the trail marked Visitors Center. Riding north from the Four Point Trail Intersection,

bikers soon encounter an unmarked trail junction (8.7). The trail straight ahead is sometimes blocked by a locked gate. If open, it soon becomes gravelly and ends in .4 mile at a footbridge which crosses a ditch to the rear of the Whittier Narrows Nature Center nature trail. *See Ride 12* for details on the nature center.

By turning left at the intersection, bikers arrive at Durfee Avenue (8.9). Turn east on Durfee, ride .1 mile and cross Durfee into the parking lot for Legg Lake. The lake lies over a slope behind the parking lot. This beautiful, spacious park provides an excellent rest stop before the return trip to Santa Fe Dam.

Linking: For information on the Whittier Narrows Recreation Area and possible side trips around Legg Lake and to the park visitors center, also *see Ride 12.*

# RIDE 4

## SAN GABRIEL RIVER TRAIL

# Whittier Narrows Dam to Wilderness Park

**Distance:** 15.8 miles round trip

**General Location:** Whittier Narrows, Pico Rivera, Norwalk

**Features:** This ride begins through a verdant, wooded area of the Whittier Narrows Wildlife Sanctuary, then climbs

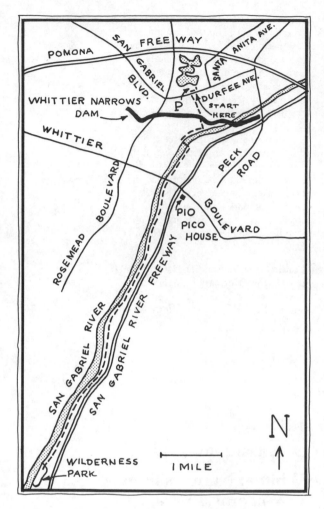

the Whittier Narrows Dam for sweeping views across the valley plain to the San Gabriel Mountains rising abruptly 11 miles to the north. The trail continues atop the river levee along a particularly beautiful section of the San Gabriel, dense with thickets of willows, rich with bird life, and uncemented. Riders

will see the multiple channels cut by the river as it works its way south through the vast gravel beds it originally deposited there. The home of Pio Pico, last governor of Mexican California, lies just over the levee at the Whittier Boulevard exit. Now a state historical park, it is a three-star stop along this segment of the trail.

**Difficulty:** Easy. When the river is in flood, the trail becomes dangerous; the entry gate is locked during high water and entry is impossible.

**Getting There:** From the Pomona Freeway (Highway 60), exit south on San Gabriel Boulevard, continuing as San Gabriel becomes Durfee Avenue. Pass the Texaco plant on the left; soon a Bike Trail sign marks the trail entry on the right. Continue .1 mile and turn left into the free Legg Lake parking area. (If you reach Velsir Street or Santa Anita Avenue, you have gone too far.)

From the San Gabriel River Freeway (I-605), exit north on Peck Road. Cross the San Gabriel River; turn west on Durfee. Pass Velsir Street and turn right into the Legg Lake parking area.

**Finding the Trail:** From the parking lot, ride west .1 mile on Durfee. The trail enters the wildlife sanctuary through an opening in a long chain link fence on the south side of Durfee. A sign on the fence gives the address, 530 Durfee.

**Description:** Leaving Durfee, the trail winds through a heavily wooded and isolated section of the sanctuary. Bunnies are apt to hop across the path, and ravens caw from treetops. At the first unmarked intersection (.2 mile), turn

right. The left road is sometimes open, sometimes closed with a chain link gate. If open, it makes an intersting diversion (.8 mile round trip) along a gravel road to a footbridge which crosses a slough to the rear of the Whittier Narrows Nature Center. A nature walking trail leads by a small lake and posted nature exhibits. If you wish to explore, lock your bikes and leave them at the bridge. They are not allowed on the nature trail.

Returning to the intersection, ride south to the Four Point Trail Intersection.

**Linking:** Here trails radiate in all directions. The trail marked Upper Rio Hondo Bike Route Begin is actually a spur that links the San Gabriel River Trail to both the Upper Rio Hondo Trail (*Ride 8*) and the Lario Trail (*Ride 9.*) The trail turning north along the San Gabriel follows the river to the base of the San Gabriel Mountains (32.4 miles round trip). *See Rides 2 and 3.*

Our trail turns south toward the Whittier Narrows Dam. Before reaching the dam it crosses a runoff channel from the river. When the river is high, the runoff flows directly across the trail, which crosses the outlet on a cement path poured on top of piled of rocks that serve as a coffer dam for the runoff. I've watched a number of people hesitate at this point because it looks unsafe to ride through a hundred feet of flowing water. The only danger is in going too fast and getting wet shoes from the wave the bicycle wheels wash up. Heavy piles of debris clinging to the fence posts along the upper side of the trail testify to the strength of the river when it is in flood.

The trail climbs 56 feet up the side of the dam, then drops down the dam face to continue on the river's west levee.

Splendid views may be had from the top of the dam by taking a side trip (2 miles round trip) along the crest of the dam to Rosemead Boulevard. The final section of the dam, west from Rosemead, is usually shut off by a locked gate; if it happens to be open, riders may continue across the dam, cross the outlet of the Rio Hondo, and drop down the south face of the dam to pick up the Lario Trail.

The dam is 3.3 miles long; its crest is 239 feet above sea level and 56 feet above the river. Completed in 1956, it drains 554 square miles; the reservoir covers 2,470 acres (most of it usually dry). Like the Santa Fe Dam, it was built to control flooding of the Rio Hondo and San Gabriel. Although the rivers are dry washes in summer, 165,000 gallons of water per second poured down the San Gabriel on March 2, 1938.

A wire cage encloses the trail as it drops down the south face of the dam. The cage prevents stray golf balls from beaning riders as they pass the Pico Rivera Municipal Golf Course. At 1.5 miles the trail turns east and crosses the river on the San Gabriel River Parkway to the east levee, where it remains all the way to Long Beach.

The trail crosses under Beverly Boulevard (2.2) and the Union Pacific railroad tracks (2.4). An intriguing sign painted on the trail at 2.8 miles states: Halfway. I have never been able to figure out what it is halfway to. The next undercrossing is at Whittier Boulevard (3.0). Here we exit on the south side of Whittier and ride east 1 block to the Pio Pico State Historic Park.

In Mexican California, governorships were won by revolution, not votes. Pio Pico led three revolutions during his career, with a score of 2 wins and 1 loss. He first held the governorship in 1832 for a month, when a counter-revolution forced his resignation. His second term in office began in 1845 and was ended by the Bear Flag Revolt a year later. Pico had been born at the Mission San Gabriel; when he became governor he moved the state capital to Los Angeles and speeded up the secularization of the mission lands.

His political dealings brought him wealth and power. The small state historic park is all that is left of his extensive land holdings, which at one time included 220,000 acres scattered throughout California. The largest ranch, Santa Margarita, was 133,440 acres; the rancho is now the home of the commanding general of Camp Pendleton.

Following the Mexican-American War, Pio Pico, who had gone to Mexico, unsuccessfully to enlist aid, returned to California and acquired the 9,000 acre Rancho Paso de Bartolo, which he called affectionately *El Ranchito*. In 1852 he built the home now open to visitors. It is a pleasant two story ranch house furnished with some choice pieces of early California furniture. One room has been made into a small museum with interesting historical pictures and artifacts. The park, at 6003 Pioneer Boulevard, is open Wednesday through Sunday 10 to 5. Tours are conducted through the mansion from 1 to 3:30. Adult admission is 50 cents; children, 25 cents. Groups of 10 or more should make reservations by calling (818) 695-1217. Governor Pico, by the way, was a flamboyant character. The gold head of his cane was in the shape of a woman's leg.

Returning to the river, bikers ride south on the trail, which is now sandwiched between the San Gabriel and the Union Pacific railroad tracks. It's not unusual to see a big freight train rolling by less than 50 feet away. The trail crosses under Washington Boulevard (4.8), Slauson Avenue and the Atchison, Topeka and Santa Fe railroad tracks (5.8). Past Telegraph Road (6.8), bikers arrive at Santa Fe Springs Park; an exit is located at the south end of the park. Water and rest rooms are available as well as a playground and barbecue stoves.

Continuing south, the trail crosses under the Santa Ana Freeway and Florence Avenue (7.7) and soon arrives at Wilderness Park (7.9). The park exit is to the south of the clubhouse. A pleasant lake, full of ducks and surrounded by grassy knolls, makes this a lovely park in which to stroll, eat a bag lunch and feed the ducks.

**Linking:** Continuing south on the San Gabriel River Trail, bikers may add a loop of 16.8 miles by riding to El Dorado Park. *See Ride 5.*

The return trip is by the same route in reverse.

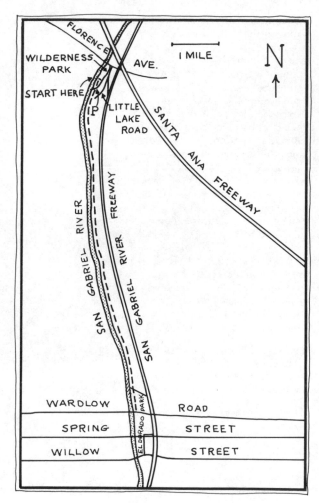

# RIDE 5

### SAN GABRIEL RIVER TRAIL

# Wilderness Park to El Dorado Park

**Distance:** 16.8 miles round trip

**General Location:** Downey, Norwalk, Cerritos, Long Beach

**Features:** This ride follows the San Gabriel River between two beautiful parks. The trail itself has no spectacular scenery and passes no interesting landmarks. But it is usually empty and is an excellent choice for cyclists who simply like to get on their bikes and ride.

**Difficulty:** Easy

**Getting There:** From the San Gabriel River Freeway (I-605), exit west on Florence Avenue. Directly west of the freeway, turn south onto Little Lake Road, which is also the entrance to the freeway going south. Before heading up onto the freeway, turn right onto Little Lake. Park free in the lot at Wilderness Park.

From the Santa Ana Freeway (I-5), exit west on Florence Avenue. Directly west of the San Gabriel Freeway, turn south onto Little Lake Road. Follow parking instructions above.

**Finding the Trail:** From the parking lot ride around the south end of the clubhouse and follow the path to the levee. Ride south on the trail.

**Description:** The beauty of the San Gabriel River bed, with its banks of willows and twining channels, soon ends; in .5 mile the cementing of the entire river channel and its levees begins. From this point the pleasures of the ride come less from views of the emasculated river running down its sorry cement ditch than from the small surprises discovered along the trail: a clump of prickly pear, a flock of chickens running loose beside the path busy pecking away at bugs, and some marvelous folk art 3.5 miles down the trail. The "Calico General Store" and the "Calico Airfield" face the bike path: a skeleton airplane with a revolving propellor sits on the runway, waiting to take off; near it, a curvaceous lady wearing only a black corset stands watching the passersby.

Three street crossings interrupt the trail. At Firestone Boulevard (3.2), bikers must leave the trail, cross the street, and return to the trail. Firestone is a wide street with heavy traffic: the crossing should be made with extreme caution. A second crossing offers a choice. Although there is no official underpass at Artesia Boulevard (7.1), it is possible to get off one's bike, scrunch down, and wheel the bike under Artesia. The alternative is to leave the path and cross Artesia, another busy highway. A third street crossing is required at 183rd Street (7.7).

Liberty Park is located directly south of South Street (8.2), and River Park, with extensive facilities for horseback riders, is located at 9.8 miles. The trail arrives at El Dorado Park and appears to end abruptly at Wardlow Street (8.5), where bikers must exit the path into the park. The path, however, is bisected within the park by both Wardlow and Spring streets. This ride ends at Wardlow, but bikers may wish to explore the many attractions, including a nature center, within El Dorado Park. *See Ride 30* for a full description of the park.

**Linking:** To follow the San Gabriel River Trail on its final segment to the Pacific Ocean (10.8 miles round trip), bikers should ride south on the peripheral road of the park under the Wardlow Tunnel and continue south, again riding under the Spring Street Tunnel. On the south side of the tunnel, ride west up the levee to regain the bike trail. *See Ride 6.*

The Billie Boswell Bicycle Path, which circles two large lakes in El Dorado Park, is described in Ride 30. The park trail utilizes the Wardlow Street undercrossing. Follow the trail north as it emerges from the tunnel.

The return trip is by the same trail in reverse.

# RIDE 6

### SAN GABRIEL RIVER TRAIL

# El Dorado Park to the Pacific Ocean

**General Location:** Long Beach

**Distance:** 10.8 miles round trip

**Features:** One of the most pleasant segments of the San Gabriel River Trail, this ride follows the San Gabriel from spacious, pastoral El Dorado Park to the river outlet at the Long Beach marina and public beach. The river, cemented for 1.5 miles of the ride, opens into a natural streambed harboring large flocks of pelicans, seagulls and egrets.

**Difficulty:** Easy

**Getting There:** From the San Diego Freeway (I-405), exit north on Palos Verdes Avenue. Drive .9 mile and turn east on Spring Street. Park free on the street just west of the bridge crossing the San Gabriel River, or continue on Spring across the bridge and turn south into the park entrance (parking is $2).

From the San Gabriel River Freeway (I-605), exit west on Willow Street (Willow becomes Katella Avenue at the Orange County border). Continue on Willow, then turn north on Studebaker Road and east on Spring Street. Follow parking instructions above.

**Finding the Trail:** From the northwest corner of the parking lot ride west toward the river levee on the park road that parallels Spring. Trail access is by a path up the levee just before the road turns north to pass under Spring through a tunnel. Ride south on the trail to begin this trip.

*Note:* Spring Street bisects the San Gabriel River trail. The trail leaves the levee north of Spring, crosses under it via a tunnel, then regains the levee. Riders who have entered the park on the north side of Spring should turn west just past the entrance kiosk and follow the road, turning south through the tunnel under Spring, then ride up the levee to begin the trip.

Bikers who have parked outside the park on Spring must enter the park (bicycles and riders free) to gain access to the trail. There is no access from Spring itself.

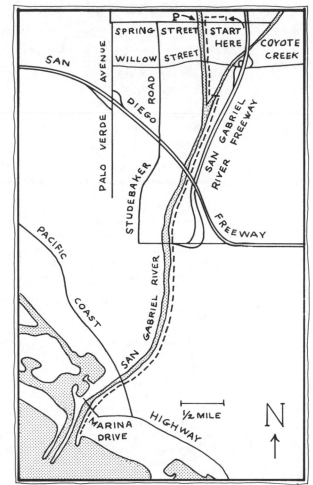

**Description:** The wild Nature Study Area of El Dorado Park borders the path on the east, and across the river the El Dorado Park golf course borders the west levee. After crossing under Willow Street (0.5), the trail arrives at the conjunction of the San Gabriel River and Coyote Creek (1.1). Here it turns abruptly east across a footbridge spanning the creek (another cemented waterway), then regains the levee to continue south. Soon, however, the cement ends. Bikers and strollers can be seen climbing and sitting on the large boulders at the demarcation zone (1.5). Access is from the other side of the river or down a steep, cemented levee wall. The trail crosses under the San Diego Freeway at its interchange with the San Gabriel River Freeway, then, at 2.7 miles, passes under the end of the San Gabriel River Freeway.

The river channel is now full and deep with tide marks on the bridge pilings implanted in it. The trail passes the huge, imposing Haynes Steam Plant, spread out on both sides of the river. The plant is run by the Los Angeles Department of Water and Power. After riding under the Pacific Coast Highway (4.5 miles), riders will see the Long Beach Marina across the river.

Bikes must be lifted over an entrance barrier at Marina Drive (5 miles). Crossing Marina, the trail continues .4 mile to the beach, where riders will find rest rooms, dressing rooms and bike racks. Swimming or sunning on the beach provides a pleasant interlude before the return trip. Or riders may explore the shops and restaurants in Shoreline Village by crossing the river on Marina, then turning south into the development.

**Linking:** This ride may be extended by a tour through the island community of Naples. To get there, ride northeast on Marina from the west end of the bridge across the San Gabriel. Follow Marina to Westminster, turn west and cross the bridge into Naples. *See Ride 31.*

On the return trip to El Dorado Park, watch for the footbridge crossing Coyote

Creek. Another bike trail continues straight up Coyote Creek into Orange County and it is easy to miss the turn.

**Linking:** After returning to El Dorado Park, riders may wish to ride the extensive trails in the park or explore the nature center and nature walk. *See Ride 30.*

# UPPER RIO HONDO BIKE TRAIL

The power of this apparently modest stream, which jumped its banks in the winter of 1867–68 and formed the new San Gabriel River, is not evident as bikers follow its cemented channel from the headwaters at Peck Road Water Conservation Lake to its confluence with the Los Angeles River. However, the potential force of the Rio Hondo can be gauged by the fact that during one 24-hour period in January 1943, 26 inches of rain fell at Hogee's Camp in Big Santa Anita Canyon, only one of three channels that drain into the Rio Hondo. Little Santa Anita and Sawpit Wash are the other two.

Two rides follow the Rio Hondo to the Whittier Narrows Dam. South of the dam the Lario Trail continues along the river levee.

**Ride 7.** Peck Road Water Conservation Park to Whittier Narrows Recreation Area. This short ride follows the Rio Hondo to the Whittier Narrows, where the river runs free through the beautiful bottomland.

**Ride 8.** Whittier Narrows Recreation Area to Grant Rea Park. Another short ride, this trail crosses several flowing creeks in the prettiest section of the bottomland, then climbs Whittier Dam to Grant Rea Park.

# RIDE 7

UPPER RIO HONDO BIKE TRAIL

## Peck Road Water Conservation Park to Whittier Narrows Recreation Area

**Distance:** 9.4 miles round trip

**General Location:** El Monte, South El Monte

**Features:** Starting at a lake formed at the confluence of the Santa Anita and Sawpit Washes, this ride is the first section of a trail that follows the Rio Hondo from its headwaters here to its confluence with the Los Angeles River. The ride crosses a beautiful area in the Whittier Narrows, where the Rio Hondo is let loose from its cement corset to run free through the Narrows. This trail is virtually unknown and rarely used. It is a good ride for bikers who like a speedy, unobstructed run.

**Difficulty:** Easy

**Getting There:** From the San Bernardino Freeway (I-10), exit north on Peck Road. Drive 2.3 miles. About one block past Celine Street (on left), turn left into parking lot for the Peck Road Water Conservation Park.

From the San Gabriel River Freeway (I-605), exit west on Lower Azusa Road. Drive 1.3 miles to Peck Road. Turn north on Peck and follow instructions above for parking.

From the Foothill Freeway (I-210), exit south on Myrtle Avenue. Drive 1.5 miles to the end of Myrtle at Peck Road. Continue south on Peck .8 mile; turn right into parking for the Peck Road Water Conservation Park.

**Finding the Trail:** Wheel bikes across a stretch of dirt at the west end of the parking lot onto an access road running along the south edge of the lake. Ride west to the trail.

**Description:** The water conservation lake, dammed at its south end, is a popular fishing area; and bikers will share the parking lot with fisher people heading for the lake with their folding chairs and poles. An amazing assortment of fish have been pulled out of the lake, including red ear sunfish, channel catfish, bullhead catfish, black crappie, bluegill, large mouth bass, thread fin shad, and even rainbow trout.

The trail follows the east levee of the Rio Hondo. The river bed is completely cemented; and the first point of scenic interest along the trail is the El Monte Airport. The trail parallels the runway, and a rest area (0.8) with benches allows bikers to watch the small planes land and take off. For fun you can ride further along the trail and see a plane take off directly over your head.

After crossing under the Southern Pacific railroad tracks, bikers arrive at Pioneer Park (1.9), where they will find

broad shade trees, an exercise par course, picnic tables and rest rooms.

The RTD Park 'n' Ride bus terminal also has a rest area with tables, benches, and a welcome water fountain. A third rest stop can be made at Fletcher Park (2.3); a second entry to the park is just west of the San Bernardino Freeway, which the trail crosses under at the park.

At 4.5 miles a spur (.1) to the right leads to an overlook where the Rio Hondo enters the Whittier Narrows and is no longer paved. The contrast is extraordinary. To the north is a barren, concrete-lined channel with a trickle of water running down the center. South is a wild river, cutting tiny gullies and new channels, winding in and out of willow banks, alive, murmuring.

Returning to the main trail, riders continue through the Narrows, veering away from the Rio Hondo, and complete the ride by arriving at the intersection of Rush Street and Loma Avenue at the north end of the Narrows recreation area (4.7).

**Linking:** Two options allow bikers to continue their ride. A round trip loop of 8.2 miles takes riders through the beautiful, wild bottomland of the Narrows to the Whittier Narrows Dam and Grant Rea Park. To find the trail, ride counter-clockwise on the park peripheral road. Watch for a Bike Trail sign on the right to the Lario Trail. *See Ride 8.*

A second alternative leads to Legg Lake, where bikers may follow a pleasant 2.7 mile loop around the lake. The Pomona Freeway bisects the Whittier Narrows, and to reach Legg Lake, bikers must pass over the freeway. To reach the lake, take the peripheral road counter-

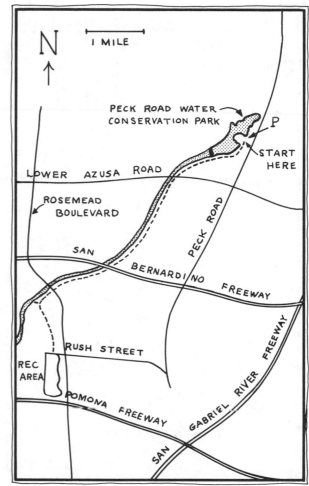

clockwise around the park, passing the Bike Trail entry sign. Exit the park on the east side to Rosemead Boulevard. Ride south on Rosemead .5 mile over the Pomona Freeway, then turn west into the park at the first parking area. Ride to the lake and pick up the bike trail. *See Ride 12.*

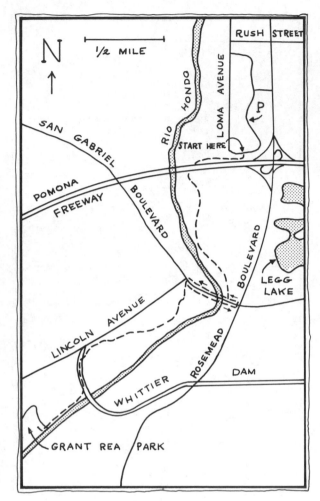

Returning to the Peck Road Park by the same trail in reverse, riders will find a magnificent view of the San Bernardino Mountains directly in front of them as they ride north. On a smog-free day the sight is spectacular.

# RIDE 8

## UPPER RIO HONDO BIKE TRAIL

# Whittier Narrows Recreation Area to Grant Rea Park

**Distance:** 8.2 miles round trip

**General Location:** Whittier Narrows

**Features:** This trail winds through some of the prettiest bottomland in the Narrows, passing several flowing creeks and a number of busily pumping oil wells, incongruous amidst the lush greenery. Although the path is part of the Rio Hondo Bike Trail, it doesn't go near the river until it climbs the back face of Whittier Dam, where cyclists will have splendid views of the luxuriant growth in the bottomland below as well as the San Gabriel Mountains to the north. The ride ends in Grant Rea Park, which has a charming barnyard zoo. You can buy fresh eggs there if the chickens are laying.

**Difficulty:** Easy. One climb up Whittier Narrows Dam.

**Getting There:** From the Pomona Freeway (Highway 60), exit north on Rosemead Boulevard. North of the freeway, turn west from Rosemead into free parking for Whittier Narrows Recreation Area A.

From the San Bernardino Freeway (I-10), exit south on Rosemead Boulevard. Drive about 2 miles and turn west into free parking for Whittier Narrows Recreation Area A.

**Finding the Trail:** Two trails leave from the peripheral road which encircles this section of the Whittier Narrows. The northern half of the Upper Rio Hondo Trail leaves from the northern end of the park and follows the Rio Hondo north (*see Ride 7*). To find the trail described in this ride, peddle to the southwest area of the peripheral road. Watch for the Bike Route sign on the south side of the road. Follow the access trail to the bike path.

**Description:** The trail parallels the Pomona Freeway for .3 mile. Since the path is built at the level of the freeway, it provides a different vantage point from which to view the flow of traffic—not in it, but with it. After crossing under the freeway, the trail winds through some beautiful, unspoiled bottomland, crosses a rushing stream (.6), and emerges from the Narrows at San Gabriel Boulevard (1.1)

**Linking:** This section of San Gabriel Boulevard links the Rio Hondo, Lario and San Gabriel River bike trails.

Additional loops of 16.8 miles round trip north to Santa Fe Dam or 14.8 miles round trip south to Wilderness Park begin at the San Gabriel River Bike Trail intersection. To get there, ride southeast on San Gabriel Boulevard to its intersection with Rosemead Boulevard (0.1). Cross to the southeast corner of the intersection. Enter a service road that angles slightly south from San Gabriel by lifting bicycles over an entrance barrier. Follow the service road to the Four Point Trail Intersection (0.9). *See Rides 3 and 4.*

To continue on the Upper Rio Hondo Bike Trail, ride northwest on San Gabriel across the Rio Hondo. Cross San Gabriel with the light at Lincoln Avenue (1.3). The trail angles south on an access road (with entrance barrier) between Lincoln and San Gabriel. For the next 1.1 miles the trail passes through another lush section of the bottomland where oil wells pump busily among the bushes.

Leaving the bottomland, the trail climbs Whittier Narrows Dam to a parking area at the crest of the dam (2.4). This dam, like the Santa Fe Dam to the northeast, was built for flood control by the Los Angeles District of the U.S. Army Corps of Engineers. It contains the floodwaters of both the Rio Hondo and San Gabriel Rivers, which merge behind the dam in high water. The earth-filled dam is more than 3 miles long. Its crest is 239 feet above sea level and 56 feet above the rivers. Completed in 1956, it drains an area of 554 square miles and controls a reservoir of 2,470 acres.

A sign at the parking area reads Entry Lario Trail and displays a bike trail map showing distances along the trail as well as entry points.

After enjoying the sweeping views from the dam crest, riders should lift bikes over the low barrier fence and ride out along the dam. The eastern half of the dam between Rosemead and the San Gabriel River is open to bikers. However, the road abruptly ends at a locked gate. Bikers should turn south and descend the face of the dam at the first service road (2.6).

After descending the dam, the trail gains the west levee of the Rio Hondo and follows it .2 mile to a bridge across the equestrian trail running parallel to the bike path. Our ride takes the bridge west to Grant Rea Park.

The Barnyard Zoo is a special attraction at the park. To ride to it, bikers skirt the ball field, keeping it on their left, then ride to the south end of the parking lot. The zoo, built by the Soroptomist Club of Montebello in 1969, is a fine red barn full of farm animals, including a cow, goats, sheep, horse, geese, a Shetland pony, and even a big turtle. The zoo is open 1 to 5 weekdays and noon to 5 weekends during the school year; closed Christmas and New Year's Day. During summer vacation, hours are noon to 5 daily. The zoo sells fresh eggs at 75 cents a dozen when available (bring your own carton). Weekends 1 to 4 children may take a pony cart ride for 50 cents. Youngsters enjoy a seasonal visit to see the turkeys before Thanksgiving.

**Linking:** An additional loop of 18 miles round trip continues south on the Lario Trail past the confluence of the Rio Hondo and Los Angeles River to Hollydale Park. *See Ride 9.*

Bikers return by the same route. At the intersection of San Gabriel and Lincoln, the trail follows the west side of San Gabriel to Rosemead, then crosses the street and returns to the trail intersection on the east side of San Gabriel.

# LARIO TRAIL

The 21 mile Lario Trail follows the Rio Hondo and Los Angeles River to the Pacific Ocean. Seven parks lie next to the river levees, providing sensible

stopping points for bikers looking for short rides. The trail is lightly traveled and has only three street crossings, all within a mile, offering fine open stretches for bikers who want a fast, safe trail.

The trail is divided into two rides.

**Ride 9.** Whittier Narrows Dam to Hollydale Park. Offering extensive views of the Narrows bottomland from the dam, the 9.5 mile ride follows the Rio Hondo to the Los Angeles River.

**Ride 10.** Hollydale Park to Long Beach Harbor. A moderate ride, this trip follows the Los Angeles River to its outlet in Long Beach near delightful Shoreline Park.

# RIDE 9

## LARIO TRAIL

# Whittier Narrows Dam to Hollydale Park

**Distance:** 19 miles round trip to Hollydale Park; 12.8 miles round trip to John Anson Ford Regional Park

**General Location:** Montebello, Downey, Bell Gardens, and Hollydale

**Features:** Panoramic views of the wild bottomland behind the Whittier Narrows Dam and of the San Gabriel Mountains rising abruptly 13 miles away provide a splendid beginning for this

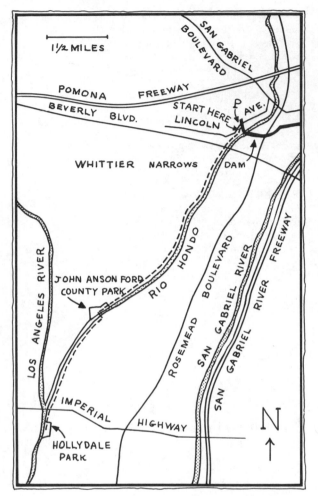

of the two rivers. A pleasant respite from urban planning run amok is provided by a stop at Hollydale Park before the return ride.

**Difficulty:** Easy

**Getting There:** From the Pomona Freeway (Highway 60), exit south on San Gabriel Boulevard and drive .7 mile. Turn south on Lincoln Avenue; drive .8 mile and park at the dam view site.

From the San Gabriel River Freeway (I-605), exit west on Beverly Boulevard. Turn north on Rosemead Boulevard, west on San Gabriel Boulevard and south on Lincoln. Drive .8 mile and park at the dam view site.

From the San Bernardino Freeway (I-10), exit south on Walnut Grove Avenue. Continue south as Walnut Grove merges with San Gabriel. Turn south on Lincoln, drive .8 mile and park at the dam view site.

**Finding the Trail:** To enter the Lario Trail, lift bicycles over the low fence between the parking lot and dam. Ride out along the top arch of the dam and follow the first road leading down the face of the dam. If you continue along the top of the dam, the path ends at a locked gate at .1 mile. From the parking lot a second path, the Upper Rio Hondo Trail, descends the backside of the dam on an unmarked service road with barrier entrance. *See Ride 8.*

**Description:** Leaving the dam, the trail descends to the west levee of the Rio Hondo. An equestrian trail parallels the bike path, and the first exit from the path (.6) is across a bridge spanning the

horse trial; the exit leads to Grant Rea Park, a delightful small park with a barnyard zoo where visitors may inspect sheep, goats, chickens, and turkeys. (*See Ride 8* for a full description.) As the trail continues south, a second exit at the south end of Grant Rea (1.0) leads to Beverly Boulevard. In quick succession the trail passes under Whittier Boulevard (1.5) and swings sharply west off the levee to cross the Union Pacific railroad tracks. For the next 3 miles the trail descends and ascends the levee twice. A painted line along the center of the trail guides bikers through puzzling turns. At the railroad tracks a small bridge leads across a rushing outlet from the river (1.7). Just beyond the outlet are a table, benches, water fountain and shade tree, providing a pleasant site from which to watch the flowing stream. Until this point, the Rio Hondo has been full of water; but here the water disappears into a spreading basin. These basins, dotting the county, are used to return river water to the ground, where it sinks and raises the level of the underground water table. Riders may wonder at the bizarre sensation of riding beside a huge, cemented river channel that is empty while beside it a free flowing creek rolls merrily along. Signs warn bikers to stay away from the creek: it is treated sewage water. It's a pretty scene, nevertheless.

The trail next crosses under Washington Boulevard (2.9), where a pleasant rest stop has a shaded bench, view of the creek and a water fountain. A trail exit is available by crossing the creek and peddling south up the embankment to Bluff Road. The trail follows the auxiliary creek to Sycamore Street (3.7), where it swings east and regains the levee.

trip. The trail passes several beautiful runoff channels of the Rio Hondo as well as some of the most barren and unrelenting stretches of industrial blight in Los Angeles. Uncounted tons of concrete were used to cement the Rio Hondo and Los Angeles River; much of that cement is on view at the confluence

The trail ducks under the Atchison, Topeka and Santa Fe railroad tracks (4.2), Slauson Avenue (4.4), and the Santa Ana Freeway (4.5) in quick succession, then returns to the levee for a ride to Treasure Island Park (5.1). The park is long, thin, and fenced off from the bike trail. It can be entered through a rolled-up section of the chain link fence at the center of the park. Children will like this park. The park headquarters is built in the form of a large pirate ship with a roof deck for climbing. In case the entrance through the fence has been unrolled, there is a second entrance at the south end of the park (5.3). Take Foster Bridge Road, then go right on Bluff Road to the entrance.

The trail crosses under Florence Avenue (6.0), then arrives at John Anson Ford County Park (6.4). This pleasant shady park, with a fine small lake, swimming pool, water fountain and rest rooms, make a welcome rest stop.

Bikers taking the shorter ride should return to Whittier Dam from the park.

For those continuing south, the trail crosses the river to the east levee on a pedestrian bridge just south of the park entrance. Watch for the bridge. Even though the turn is marked by a line painted on the trail, it is easy to miss since the service road continues straight south on the levee beside the park(and it dead-ends .7 mile later at the Southern Pacific railroad tracks).

The trail passes Crawford Park (6.9), with water, rest rooms that are sometimes locked, and a children's playground. Passing the park, the trail enters an industrial area. Bleak factories abut the river; vegetation disappears: the only life is an occasional beetle crawling across the path. The trail passes under Firestone Boulevard (7.2); a fascinating passenger car that crosses the river on a cable high above the river provides a break in the grim landscape. It's locked, so no one can try it.

In quick succession the trail crosses under Southern Avenue (7.5), Eastern Avenue (7.9), and the Union Pacific railroad tracks, finally arriving at the confluence of the Rio Hondo and the Los Angeles River near Imperial Highway (8.5).

A view of the two rivers may be had from the pedestrian walkway on the bridge spanning the river at Imperial. To reach the walkway, exit the bike path on the north side of Imperial. The sterile concrete troughs of these rivers are a barren contrast to the wooded, life-filled bottomland where the Rio Hondo and San Gabriel River have been allowed to run free.

These free-flowing rivers are not tidy. When in flood they tear out bushes and trees willy-nilly, cut away entire banks of vegetation and deposit mud and rock in their wake as they recede. Perhaps it is our human desire for order—as well as greed—that underlies the urge to cement our rivers into place. A free-flowing river confounds map makers and engineers, prime guardians of order in our universe. It is difficult to map a river when its channel changes course each winter. We could have had the rivers and flood control, too, if our planners had not insisted on building to the very edge of the channels but had left the rivers space in which to move. Los Angeles could have had a mile-wide park running from the San Gabriel Mountains to the ocean instead of these sterile concrete basins. In Sacramento, parts of Discovery Park, at the confluence of the Sacramento and American rivers, flood each winter; summertime, at low water, it is a beautiful park. Until the people who live in cities demand their environment be made beautiful and livable, landscapes like this confluence will proliferate.

**Linking:** An extended loop ride is available from this point. The Los Angeles River Trail, 6.4 miles round trip, follows the west levee of the Los Angeles River. Cross the river on the pedestrian walkway on the north side of the bridge, then turn north at the Bike Trail sign onto the levee. *See Ride 11.*

Returning to the bike path, riders continue south .8 mile to Hollydale Park (9.3). An exit at the south end of the park, where bikers will find rest rooms and water, marks the end of the trip.

**Linking:** The final segment of the Lario Trail continues from Hollydale Park to the ocean in Long Beach, a round trip of 23.7 miles. *See Ride 10.*

The return to Whittier Dam is on the same trail in reverse.

# RIDE 10

## LARIO TRAIL

# Hollydale Park to Long Beach Harbor

**Distance:** 23.6 miles round trip

**General Location:** South Gate, Paramount, Long Beach

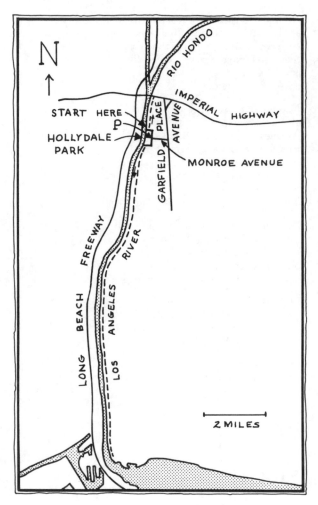

N

START HERE

HOLLYDALE
PARK

RIO HONDO

IMPERIAL

HIGHWAY

GARFIELD    AVENUE    PLACE

MONROE AVENUE

LONG    BEACH    FREEWAY

LOS    ANGELES    RIVER

2 MILES

**Features:** This ride, the final link in the Lario Trail, follows the Los Angeles River from its confluence with the Rio Hondo to the Pacific Ocean. Passing several pleasant parks and numerous corrals and stables, the trail utilizes the maintenance road atop the broad, high river levee; it allows sweeping views of the river, the Long Beach skyline and Vincent Thomas Bridge.

**Difficulty:** Easy. Headwinds off the ocean blow in the afternoon.

**Getting There:** Take the Long Beach Freeway (Highway 7) to South Gate and exit east on Imperial Highway. Turn south at the first light, Garfield Place; then turn west on Monroe Avenue at the sign to Hollydale Park. Park free in the parking lot at the park.

**Finding the Trail:** A short asphalt path leaves the south end of the parking lot and leads to a trail access entrance through the chain link fence along the river levee. Follow the access north up the levee to the Lario Trail.

**Description:** Ride north .8 mile for a view of the confluence of the Rio Hondo and Los Angeles River. A trickle of water runs down a concrete ditch sunk in the middle of each of these two vast, sterile concrete channels, exemplifying urban planning at its worst. Compare this barren landscape with the wooded bottomland where the Rio Hondo and San Gabriel merge.

**Linking:** The ride may be extended 6.4 miles round trip by biking the Los Angeles River Trail. Exit the bike path on the north side of Imperial (just south of the confluence), cross the river on the pedestrian path located on the north side of the bridge, and enter the bike path at the west end of the bridge, riding north along the river's west levee. The entry point is marked by a Bike Trail sign.

After viewing the confluence, bikers turn south and head for Long Beach. If the river channel is dry, an interesting alternative route between Imperial and the railroad tracks .7 mile south is available. At Imperial take the steep access road to the concrete floor of the river bed and ride south next to the flowing ditch in the center of the river bed. This provides a closeup view of what is left of the Los Angeles River. Return to the top of the levee at the railroad overpass.

An interesting conundrum presents itself at the first three street crossings: Rosecrans Avenue (2.0), Compton Boulevard (2.7), and Alondra Boulevard (3.2). Signs plainly warn riders not to cross on the road but to descend to the river bed and cross under the street. However, the river often overflows its ditch along this stretch and covers the bike crossings with a mix of water, mud and debris. Riding a bike through this mess is unpleasant at best and downright dangerous if the river is high enough. Most riders ignore the signs and cross the streets, which is also a hazardous undertaking. These streets are divided and carry fast-moving, heavy traffic. Experienced bikers avoid either alternative by riding over the edge of the levee and making the crossing on the steep levee wall. If you want to try this, ride down to the river bed and practice on the lower edge of the levee first, or you may find both yourself and your bike tumbling down the levee.

Starting at Imperial, an equestrian path parallels the bike trail. Bikers can expect to see horseback riders. Horses are corraled along the route, and there are equestrian rings at Hollydale Park and between Alondra and Atlantic Avenue; riders may chance upon practice sessions or a competition.

If bikers need to catch their breath after hustling across Rosecrans, they will find a long, narrow recreation area with the marvelous name of Banana Park stretching between Rosecrans and Compton. An access path leaves the levee at 3.2 miles. The park has bike racks, water and a children's playground.

Leaving the park and crossing Compton (2.7) and Alondra (2.3), bikers will cross under Atlantic Avenue (3.5) and the Artesia Freeway (4.0). The exit to De Forest Park leaves the path at 5 miles; a rest room is located at the south end of the park. The park is a pleasant stopping point for riders who want a shorter round trip.

As the trail nears the ocean, the landscape flattens and opens out. Compton Creek enters the river from the west (6.7), and brush surrounds a field of pumping oil wells (7.3) as the trail approaches the sand bars, boulders and huge chunks of cement that mark the division between the cemented and natural river bed (9.1).

As riders cross under the Pacific Coast Highway (10.0) and Anaheim Street (10.6), the river, influenced by the ocean tides, is no longer a trickle but a massive body of water. The Vincent Thomas Bridge to the west dominates the landscape, and riders soon arrive at the gate marking the end of the Lario Trail (11.8 miles).

**Linking:** A short ride will take bikers to Shoreline Park with views of the Queen Mary and Long Beach Marina. Bike trails in the park add a 5.9 mile loop to the trip. To reach Shoreline Park, leave the trail and ride east through the parking lot on the marked bike trail. *See Ride 29 for details.*

The return trip is by the same path in reverse, and with the wind at their backs, bikers will float along the trail.

# LOS ANGELES RIVER BIKE TRAIL

On Christmas Day, 1889, the Los Angeles River, the San Gabriel River and the Rio Hondo jumped their channels during one of the worst floods Los Angeles had seen. The three rivers met in Downey, engulfed everything in their path and swept it with them to the ocean.

The rivers were violent, treacherous and unstable (even though most of the year they survived only as dry washes), and the Los Angeles River was the most unpredictable of the lot. It has changed course twice since historians recorded such things. In 1815, in what we now call downtown Los Angeles (Alameda Street at Fourth Street), the river jumped its channel and cut a new bed west to Ballona Creek, emptying into the ocean at what is now Marina del Rey. The Los Angeles River flowed west for 10 years. Then, in the winter of 1824–25, more floods cut another channel south, and the river moved to its present bed, entering the Pacific 17 miles south of Marina del Rey.

Los Angeles' central plain wasn't the only area to feel the destructive force of the river. In 1884 it made a swamp of the San Fernando Valley from Chatsworth to Glendale and washed out the Southern Pacific railroad tracks.

The Lario Trail follows the Los Angeles River south from its confluence with the Rio Hondo, but the trail north through downtown Los Angeles, past Griffith Park and through the San Fernando Valley, waits to be built. The one completed segment of the trail, described in this section, is a sorry piece of work that badly needs extending and maintenance. When completed, the Los Angeles River Bicycle Trail will follow the Los Angeles River 53 miles from the Chatsworth Reservoir to Long Beach. Construction of the trail is delayed until a right-of-way is negotiated through the extensive railroad yards in Vernon, and planners decide on a route from Griffith Park through downtown Los Angeles, where the river has no levees to provide a ready-made path. Bikers who would like to ride Los Angeles' longest river can help the project along by calling their county supervisor and expressing interest in the project.

The one completed segment of this trail is:

**Ride 11.** A short ride north from the river's confluence with the Rio Hondo to the Vernon railroad yards.

# RIDE 11

**LOS ANGELES RIVER BIKE TRAIL**

## The Confluence to Gage Street

**Distance:** 6.4 miles round trip

**General Location:** South Gate, Cudahy, Bell

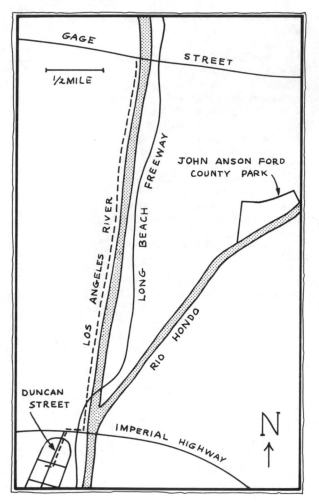

**Features:** This 3.2 mile trail along Los Angeles' longest river is so short, it seems, because planners gave it up as a bad job. Little known, neglected, liberally sprinkled with broken glass, and going nowhere, this trail should be traveled by every biker in Los Angeles. Riding it creates an abiding appreciation for any other bicycle trail in the county.

Following the west levee of the Los Angeles River from its confluence with the Rio Hondo, the trail abuts the back yards of a series of industrial plants. These yards, their fences topped with coils of barbed wire, store an incredible assortment of discarded parts, corroded pipes and rusting cans most likely full of liquids one hopes won't be emptied into the river. The river itself has been shorn of its natural beauty by the tons of cement that now line its bed. This trail should not be confused with the Lario Trail, which runs from the confluence to the ocean on the east bank of the Los Angeles River.

**Difficulty:** Easy. Both a friend and I got flat tires on the trail from unavoidable broken glass. If you want to ride this, take a broom.

**Getting There:** From the Long Beach Freeway (Highway 7), exit west on Imperial Highway. Take the first left south on Duncan Street (it is called Wright Road north of Imperial) and park on one of the side streets.

**Finding the Trail:** The trail leaves from Imperial on the Los Angeles River. To reach the trail, cross to the north side of Imperial at the light at Duncan. Ride the sidewalk east over the freeway, being especially careful when crossing the freeway entrance ramp. Follow the Bike Trail sign and ride north down to the levee before crossing the bridge over the river.

**Description:** After viewing the concrete confluence of the Los Angeles and Rio Hondo, bikers ride north along the levee.

Entrances to this trial—are at Fostoria Street, Santa Ana Street (2.0), where there is a tiny city park, Clara Street (2.3), Live Oak Street (2.5), and Florence Avenue (2.7). It's ironic that this trail, which offers so little of scenic interest, has the most extensive series of entrance gates of any of the trails in the county. The usual gap between entrances ranges from 1 to 3 miles.

The trail ends, for no apparent reason, at Gage Street (3.2). The return trip is by the same trail in reverse.

**Linking:** Bikers may ride south to the Pacific or north to Whittier Dam by crossing the river to the Lario Trail, which runs along the east banks of the Los Angeles and Rio Hondo. To enter the trail, ride east across the river by using the pedestrian walkway on the north side of Imperial. A Bike Trail sign directs riders north across a barrier entrance down onto the east levee. *See Ride 9 and Ride 10 for details.*

# BIKE LOG

# II

# The Inland Valley

*Here is a great plain, or rather a gentle slope, from the Pacific to the mountains. We are on this plain about twenty miles from the sea and fifteen from the mountains, a most lovely locality; all that is wanted naturally to make it a paradise is water, more water.*

—WILLIAM H. BREWER
  Up and Down California in 1860–1864

William H. Brewer was camped in the San Gabriel Valley in 1860 when he wrote those words, but his description serves as good advice to bicyclists today. Hot and dry in the summer, the San Gabriel Valley and the San Fernando Valley are best biked in the winter just after a rain storm has washed the air clean of smog and filled the rivers and creeks. At such moments, when the San Gabriel Mountains seem so close you can touch them and the air is like crystal, bicycle riding in Los Angeles' inland valleys is exhilarating.

Valley rides are described from east to west, starting in the San Gabriel Valley.

Other valley rides are listed in Chapter I, "The River Trails."
The rides are:

**Ride 12.** Legg Lake Loop. A short ride in the Whittier Narrows around a meandering lake.

**Ride 13.** San Gabriel Mission to the Huntington Library. Two loops, one easy, one difficult, through beautiful San Marino with stops at the mission and the Huntington Gardens.

**Ride 14.** Arcadia Loop. A long ride through Arcadia with extensive views of the immaculate gardens in Arcadia's foothill estates and a possible stop at the Los Angeles County Arboretum.

**Ride 15.** Arroyo Seco Bike Trail. A short ride along the rustic Arroyo Seco creek in South Pasadena with an extended loop including visits to Heritage Square, the Lummis Home and the Casa de Adobe.

**Ride 16.** Kenneth Newell Bikeway. A more difficult ride along the Arroyo Seco in Pasadena past the Rose Bowl and ending at the Jet Propulsion Lab. An optional sightseeing tour of the lab can be scheduled.

**Rides 17 and 18.** Griffith Park. Two loops, one level, one on hills, through the largest city park in the United States.

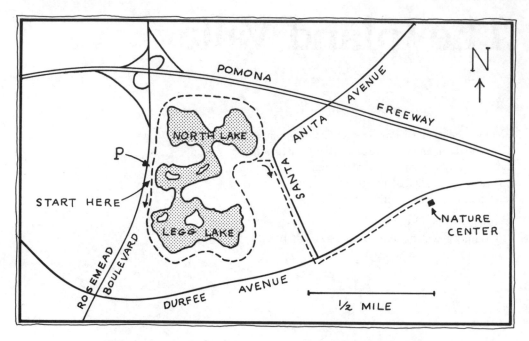

Ride 19. Sepulveda Basin Bikeway. Two popular loops around the Sepulveda Basin Recreation Area.

Ride 20. Brown's Creek Bikeway. A short ride along Brown's Creek to captivating Chatsworth Park north.

# RIDE 12

# Legg Lake Loop

**Distance:** 2.7 miles round trip, Legg Lake Loop; 3.7 miles round trip, including spur to Nature Center

**General Location:** Whittier Narrows

**Features:** This easy trail follows the meandering shoreline of Legg Lake, offering views of the lake, its islands, and a fine assortment of ducks and geese that will literally surround you when you stop for lunch. It's a perfect place to bring small children and a sack of stale bread. Facilities at the lake include two food stands (open weekends), several rest rooms, roofed picnic areas and childrens' play areas. Paddle boats may be rented weekends.

Although this short and easy ride may appeal mostly to beginning bikers, Legg Lake also connects with the Upper Rio Hondo, Lario and San Gabriel River bike trails, which radiate from it like spokes.

Cyclists may also wish to explore the area's visitors center and nature center, both within easy riding distance from Legg Lake.

The lake is located in the southern section of the Whittier Narrows Recreation Area. This 1,000 acre area is, with the exception of Griffith Park and the state parks, one of Los Angeles' largest playgrounds.

Fisher people catch catfish, bass, bluegill, and crappie in its lake.

An archery range is open early morning to sunset Wednesday through Sunday. (The rules are: bring your own bows and arrows, no crossbows, and no one under 18.)

Trap or skeet shooting lessons are offered at the firing range. They include the use of a 12- or 20-gauge shotgun. Group lessons are $9.00; private lessons are $35.00 an hour. Shooting without the lesson costs $4.25 and includes one box of 25 shells. Hours are: 6A.M. to 10P.M. Tuesday; 1 to 9 Wednesday, Thursday; 10 to 4 Saturday; and 9 to 4 Sunday.

Whittier Narrows also has six soccer fields, dog training classes, an area for radio-controlled model boat racing, and a frisbee golf course. Park headquarters are at 100 Durfee Avenue, South El Monte. Call (818) 443-0317 for information.

**Difficulty:** Easy. This hard-packed dirt path is shared with pedestrians and go-carts of all types. Ride carefully to avoid skidding in the fine gravel or mud when wet.

**Getting There:** From the Pomona Freeway (Highway 60), exit south on Rosemead. Drive to the sign that says Legg Lake Parking. Make a U-turn, then turn right into the free parking lot at the sign marked North Lake. If that lot is full, continue on the peripheral road inside the park and stop at any of the parking lots scattered around the edge of the lake.

**Finding the Trail:** At the parking lot the trail passes northeast of the restroom. Turn south to ride counterclockwise around the lake.

**Description:** Legg Lake is actually three lakes lying next to each other in the bottomland and joined by narrow waterways. The northernmost of the three is called North Lake. The bike trail follows the meandering shoreline of all the lakes, with our ride beginning on the west shore of North Lake.

It is almost impossible to get lost following the trail; however, at .4 mile a spur leading across the neck between North Lake and Legg Lake turns east (a water fountain marks the turn). Bikers should stay right and continue to Legg Lake.

At the west end of Legg Lake a 10-foot-high cement octopus surveys the lake. Be sure to walk around it to see its boggle-eyed stare. Further along a two-headed cement sea monster snakes across the grass as children climb enthusiastically on its coils.

As the trail rounds Legg Lake, it returns to the branch trail that has crossed the waterway between North Lake and Legg Lake. Bikers who want to visit the Whittier Narrows Nature Center should turn east here and follow the path to the parking lot bordering Santa Anita Avenue. Ride south .3 mile to Durfee Avenue, then turn east on Durfee and ride .2 mile. Turn right into parking for the nature center.

There are bike racks where bicycles should be securely locked while riders explore the center.

The nature center stands on the edge of a wildlife sanctuary that attempts to preserve a small part of the bottomland in a natural state. It calls itself "an island within a sea of concrete and metal." An interesting nature trail that takes about 20 minutes to walk leaves from the center and winds through the sanctuary to a large pond called Lake Aquatecos. The lake is actually artificial; it was created when the Audubon Society had tons of dirt removed to create a depression below the existing water table level in the area. Numerous migratory and resident birds use the lake, and visitors will be able to spot many species.

The nature center itself has several live native animals on display as well as wildlife exhibits and booklets describing the nature trail. The center is open 9 to 5 daily.

**Linking:** Bikers may extend their ride in several directions by biking to the Four Point Trail Intersection in the wildlife sanctuary. To reach it, continue west on Durfee .5 mile past Santa Anita. Watch for the Bike Trail sign pointing across Durfee. Enter the sanctuary through a barrier entrance in the chain link fence at 530 Durfee. *See Rides 3, 4, 8, and 9 for details.*

Cyclists should return to the Legg Lake Bike Trail by the same streets in reverse. The trail continues counterclockwise around the lake and soon returns to the parking lot.

# RIDE 13

# Arcadia Loop

**Distance:** 13.2 miles round trip, Rancho Oaks and Lucky Baldwin Loops; 16.6 miles round trip, Rancho Oaks, Lucky Baldwin and Hugo Reid Loops

**General Location:** Arcadia

**Features:** This ride follows city streets through one of the most beautiful residential areas in the county. Passing Santa Anita Race Track and the Los Angeles County Arboretum, it combines two of four posted bicycle routes in Arcadia. The longer ride adds a third loop. Although this trip incorporates 40 turns of varying degrees of obscurity, it is included because of its great beauty.

Rides on city streets should generally be taken in a clockwise direction to prevent forced left turns. This route, however, is posted only in a counterclockwise direction; anyone attempting to follow it going clockwise is assured of getting lost.

The ride is characteristic of a number of bike trails on city streets; and if you enjoy it, you may call the recreation departments in Woodland Hills, Glendale, Highland Park, Pasadena, Pico Rivera, and San Pedro, to name only a few, for information and maps.

**Difficulty:** Moderate. The route includes one steady grade into the residential areas and a series of shorter climbs over rolling slopes at the base of the San Gabriel Mountains. The ride can be ruined by heavy smog and should be attempted after rains or winds have cleaned the valley.

**Elevation Gain:** 330 feet

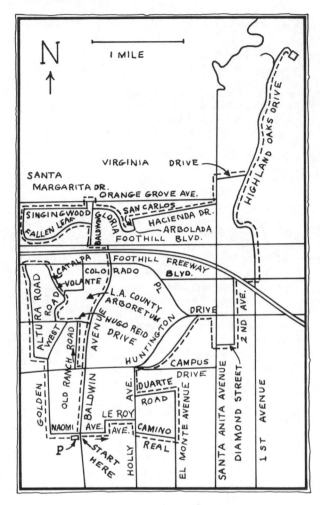

**Getting There:** From the Foothill Freeway (I-210) exit south on Baldwin Avenue. Drive about 2.2 miles and park in the lot of the small shopping center at Baldwin and Naomi Avenue.

From the San Bernardino Freeway (I-10) exit north on Santa Anita Avenue. Turn west on Valley Boulevard and north on Baldwin. Drive about 4.2 miles and park in the shopping center lot at Naomi.

**Finding the Trail:** The ride begins east on Naomi.

**Description:** Describing in detail a ride with 40 turns is excessive. Bikers should take the map and watch for Bike Trail signs, posted at each turn. The following is a general description of the ride.

The trail begins in a shopping center with a Baskin Robbins ice cream store, providing incentive for a speedy return. Passing through a neighborhood of modest homes, the route soon reaches El Monte Avenue (1.2), which has a painted bike lane extending to Duarte Road. After several more turns, the route passes the Arcadia Rose Garden, with its brilliantly hued flowers.

A Bike Trail sign directs bikers northeast on Huntington Drive (2.2) past the Arcadia Chamber of Commerce. Huntington is a heavily traveled road here with little or no shoulder. Cyclists should use the sidewalk where possible. (The City of Arcadia permits bicycling on sidewalks except in business districts or in front of public buildings where people congregate.)

Another turn takes bikers past the Arcadia County Park, then across Huntington and Colorado Boulevard (4.5).

A shady park on Second Avenue (4.6) provides a cool rest stop before the route climbs into the foothill residential area. At Virginia Drive the trail turns west along the base of the foothills.

**Linking:** Bikers looking for a strenuous workout can add a 3 mile loop to the ride by continuing north on Highland Oaks Drive instead of turning onto Virginia. The road makes a sinuous, steep ascent to Wilderness Park. This secluded, little known park is situated near the base of Big Santa Anita Canyon. Santa Anita Wash flows through the canyon, and the park, shaded with pine trees, features a nature trail with descriptions in Braille. The elevation gain to the park is an additional 330 feet in 1.5 miles, and the ride should be attempted only by bikers in excellent condition.

After turning onto Virginia, the route winds for 4.3 miles along streets bordered by elegant homes seen across broad expanses of immaculately tended lawns dotted with small flower beds spilling over with color and scent.

Crossing Foothill Boulevard (10.9), the route passes the Los Angeles County Arboretum. Across the street is Santa Anita Race Track.

The L.A. County Arboretum is a 127 acre demonstration garden with a number of interesting attractions, including Lucky Baldwin's ornate Victorian-Queen Anne home. Baldwin, the colorful Bonanza king who made his fortune in the Nevada silver mines, built the home for his fourth wife (age 16 at their marriage, as was each of his brides). The marriage ended in divorce a year later, and Baldwin transformed the house into a shrine for his third wife, Jenny Dexter. Her portrait in stained glass may be seen in one of the doors. Baldwin had purchased the Rancho Santa Anita when he arrived in Southern California and once owned 40,000 acres in the San Gabriel Valley. The mansion, built in 1885, was used in the filming of the television show "Fantasy Island."

A 45 minute tram ride which costs $1.50 takes visitors through gardens planted with flora from Australia, the Mediterranean, South America, South Africa, and North America-Asia. The plants were chosen because they do well in Southern California. A demonstration garden designed by *Sunset* Magazine gives ideas on textures and materials to use in planning a garden.

Finally, visitors may wander through the jungle garden where the original Tarzan movie was filmed.

The arboretum is open 9 to 4:30 daily except Christmas. Admission is $1.50 adults, 75 cents students of all ages; children 4 and under, free. Information: (818) 446-8251.

Leaving the arboretum, the trail continues south on Baldwin Avenue and arrives at Huntington Drive (12.4). Here the trail divides. Bikers taking the short loop should continue south on Baldwin to Naomi (13.2).

Cyclists taking the long loop should turn west on Huntington, then almost immediately north on Old Ranch Road. The trail winds through more pleasant residential neighborhoods, then returns to Naomi (16.6).

# RIDE 14

## San Gabriel Mission to the Huntington Library

**Distance:** 8.1 miles round trip, Flat Loop; 9.0 miles round trip, Hill Loop

**General Location:** San Marino, San Gabriel

**Features:** This trip combines a short bicycle ride through beautiful and exclusive San Marino with longer stops at the fourth California mission, San Gabriel Archangel, and at the Huntington with its extensive botanical gardens, art gallery and world famous library. The route follows wide streets with little to moderate usage and offers sociological insight into class separation, L.A.-style. Beautiful Lacy Park in San Marino locks its gates on weekends, assuring that the working class will stay away. Because the Huntington is open only from 1 to 4, this ride first loops south for a visit to the mission, pauses for lunch or a rest at Grapevine Park, then returns to San Marino for leisurely exploration of the extensive botanical gardens. Picnics are not permitted at the Huntington.

**Difficulty:** Easy, Flat Loop. Moderate, Hill Loop.

**Getting There:** Exit the San Bernardino Freeway (I-10) heading north on Atlantic Boulevard in Alhambra. Drive 2.5 miles and turn east on Huntington Drive for 1.5 miles. Turn north on St. Albans Road. Park at Lacy Park near the park entrance.

From the Foothill Freeway (I-210), exit south on Sierra Madre Boulevard. Drive 2.3 miles; turn west on Huntington Drive for .6 mile. Turn north on St. Albans Road. Park at Lacy Park near the park entrance.

From the Pasadena Freeway (Highway 11), exit south on Fair Oaks Avenue and drive 1 mile. Turn east on Huntington Drive. Drive 2.2 miles and turn north on St. Albans Road. Park at Lacy Park near the park entrance.

**Finding the Trail:** This is one of the few rides in the book laid out on unmarked

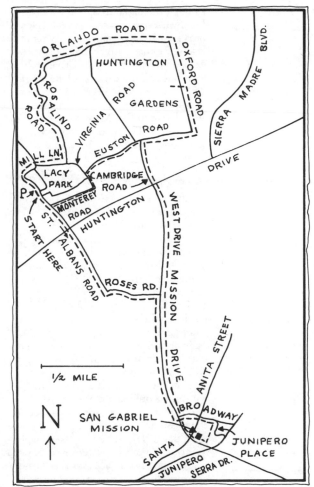

city streets. Because many of the streets in San Marino curve sharply or dead-end, it's necessary to carry a map. The ride begins south on St. Albans Street.

**Description:** San Marino is a small island of wealth and luxury surrounded by communities of modest means. St. Albans, one of the wide streets cutting through the flatlands of San Marino, is lined with spacious homes visible across broad expanses of immaculately tended lawns. Riding south on St. Albans, we cross divided Huntington Drive and continue south until St. Albans dead-ends at Roses Road. Turn east on Roses to Mission Drive (it changes name to West Drive in San Marino), then south on Mission. The modest, somewhat weathered cottages on Mission say better than any sign that we have crossed the boundary between San Marino and San Gabriel.

After crossing Las Tunas Road, continue three blocks and turn east on Broadway. Cross Santa Anita Street, then turn south at Junipero Place and ride to parking for the mission (2.8).

An Indian attack greeted the two Franciscan fathers and 14 soldiers who arrived in the San Gabriel Valley in 1771 to found a mission. To prevent a battle, as the story goes, one of the padres unfurled an oil painting of Our Lady of Sorrows whereupon the Indians put down their bows and arrows and laid beads worn about their necks in front of the picture. the original oil painting is only one of the many items of historical interest visitors may see in the mission.

Of particular interest to bikers exploring the Los Angeles waterways described in this book is the fact that the mission was moved to its present site four years after the Franciscans arrived in the valley. Flash floods alternating with summer drought caused the fathers to move the mission out of the flood plain and nearer a stable water source, Wilson Lake near San Marino.

Before the Mexican government secularized the mission in 1833, the Franciscans had built a large, complex organization. They ran 16,500 head of livestock in the valley, and approximately 6,000 Indians had been buried in the cemetery. Many had died in the smallpox and cholera epidemics in 1825. The mission church has walls five feet thick and has withstood all earthquakes in the area. By wandering through the mission and its grounds, visitors will find some sense of pioneer life in the San Gabriel Valley.

The mission is open daily 9:30 to 4:30. It is closed Good Friday, Easter, Thanksgiving and Christmas Day. A fiesta is held at the mission Labor Day weekend. Admission is $1 for adults, 50 cents for children ages 5 to 13.

Leaving the mission, bikers should follow Mission Drive around the mission to the north. Within a block is small Grapevine Park, an excellent rest stop before the return ride, which continues north on Mission Drive.

Follow Mission (becoming West Drive in San Marino) until you cross Huntington Drive (5.0); continue north on Cambridge Road to Euston Road (5.4), which forms the southern boundary of the Huntington Botanical Gardens. Ride east on Euston; turn north on Oxford Road and ride up the moderate grade to Stratford Road (6.2), where a left turn leads into the gardens.

Although car entry into the Huntington is a voluntary $2 fee, cyclists ride in free. The complex is open 1 to 4 Tuesday through Sunday.

The library exhibition hall displays a Gutenberg Bible as well as manuscripts of Benjamin Franklin's *Autobiography* and Chaucer's *Canterbury Tales*. The art gallery includes Gainesborough's *The Blue Boy* among its collection.

The gardens cover 207 acres. They include the Desert Garden, the world's largest outdoor collection of desert plants; the Jungle Garden with waterfall and tropical plants; and the Japanese Garden, a landscaped 5-acre canyon with a moon bridge, a Zen garden and a bonsai court. An entire afternoon can be spent exploring these extensive grounds.

Leaving the Huntington, the Flat Loop returns south on Oxford and west on Euston to Lacy Park. By turning south on Virginia Road, west on Monterey Road and north on St. Albans, bikers return to their cars (8.1).

The Hilly Loop leaves the Huntington north on Oxford and swings around the north boundary of the grounds west on Orlando Road. Bikers stay on Orlando as it curves around to Rosalind Road (stay right as Orlando Place splits off). Turn left on Rosalind Road and follow it to Virginia Road, being sure to stay right where Shenandoah Road splits off. Turn left on Virginia and ride to the north edge of Lacy Park. A right turn on Mill Lane takes bikers down a short, steep grade to St. Albans, where a left turn will return cyclists to their cars (9.0).

# RIDE 15

## Arroyo Seco Bike Trail

**Distance:** 4.4 miles round trip; 6.6 miles round trip including the loop to Heritage Square, the Lummis Home and the Casa de Adobe.

**General Location:** Montecito Heights, South Pasadena

**Features:** This trail drops from the bluffs along Arroyo Seco to follow a cemented bank running through the arroyo near stream level. This streambed has been paved in cobblestones rather than cement. Only in Los Angeles can you find a natural stream torn out and rebuilt to look as it looked to begin with. Both the trail, which is shaded with arching, ancient sycamores, and the Pasadena Freeway are old-fashioned, closer to nature, and more agreeable to ride than their contemporary cousins, the San Bernardino Freeway and the Los Angeles River Bike Trail.

This ride must be taken on the first or second Sunday of each month if cyclists wish to visit Heritage Square, which is open only those two days. The square houses a fascinating collection of re-stored Victorian and Queen Anne mansions hauled to the site after being scheduled for bulldozing at their old locations.

A final spur takes bikers across the Pasadena Freeway to visit El Alisal, the historic Lummis Home and the Casa de Adobe, a replica of a Spanish California hacienda typical of the 1850s.

**Difficulty:** Easy. The path has broken glass on it, pitched down from the park above, so ride carefully.

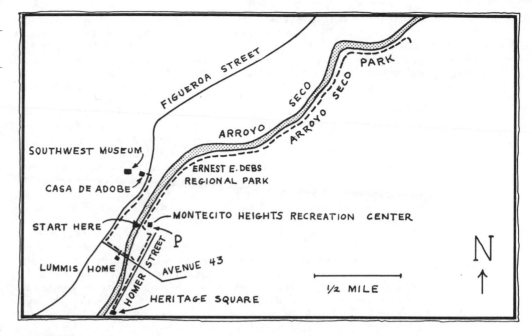

**Getting There:** Exit the Pasadena Freeway (Highway 11), east on Avenue 43. Drive 2 blocks, turn north on Homer Street and drive 1 block. Park in the free lot at the Montecito Heights Recreation Center.

**Finding the Trail:** The trail begins at the west end of the parking lot. Follow it north along the arroyo.

**Description:** Riding along the east bluff of the arroyo, cyclists will see the Pasadena Freeway across the creek. The freeway follows the arroyo all the way from Arroyo Drive to downtown Los Angeles, where the creek flows into the Los Angeles River.

**Linking:** At .3 mile the trail divides. The right fork leads to a circuitous route through Highland Park on city streets marked by Bike Trail signs. Distance of the loop, which returns to this park, is 12 miles round trip. A map for the route, which is not described in this book, is included in the map packet reviewed in the Introduction and available from the City of Los Angeles Department of Recreation and Parks.

Our ride forks left across an entrance barrier and down a short, steep grade to the bottom of the arroyo. The path follows the creek upstream. The gurgling water, sheltering trees, and solitude create a remote, peaceful country atmosphere. The trail crosses under Avenue 52 (.7), Via Marisol (1.2), where a side trail exits to Ernest E. Debs Regional

County Park above, Avenue 60 (1.4), and the Southern Pacific railroad tracks (1.6). The trail ends all too soon with an exit to the park at 2.2 miles. Bikers will find water, rest rooms and a pleasant, shaded area in which to eat lunch. Horse stables are situated at the north end of the park. Several footbridges also cross the arroyo from the park. An especially scenic bridge, located .8 mile from the trail's end, is overgrown with a beautiful hanging grape vine that turns a glorious scarlet color in the autumn.

After returning to the parking lot by the same route in reverse (4.4), bikers should ride through the lot, then pedal south on Homer Street two blocks to Heritage Square (4.9).

If bikers share my enthusiasm for old, rococo houses, a tour of Heritage Square is in order. Open from 11 to 3 the first and second Sundays of each month, admission is $1 for adults, 50 cents for seniors. Information: (213) 222-3150. The square is a repository for some of the exuberant old homes fallen victim to Los Angeles' craze for bulldozing everything in sight and building something new to replace it. At least one of the buildings here was hauled to Heritage Square literally days before being bulldozed. The goal of the Cultural Heritage Foundation, which operates 10-acre Heritage Square and offers membership to all interested persons, is to preserve historical and architectural landmarks that would otherwise be torn down.

Although many buildings in the square are still in the process of being restored, visitors may tour the inside of Hale House, where beautifully detailed restorations of the dining room, library and front parlor have been completed.

Leaving Heritage Square, bikers should ride north 1 block to Avenue 43, turn west and cross the freeway on 43rd, then turn left into the Lummis Home, El Alisal (5.5). Charles F. Lummis, founder of the Southwest Indian Museum (visible up the hill), built his home around 1895 by hand from cobblestones hauled from the Arroyo Seco streambed. According to the story, Lummis walked to California from St. Louis, Missouri, sending stories to the *Los Angeles Times* about his trip as he progressed. Arriving in Los Angeles, he went to the *Times* and was hired as city editor.

Lummis built his home in the Craftsman style then popular along the arroyo, which at the turn of the century was a center for artists and writers. A state historical landmark, the home is open 1 to 4 Wednesday through Sunday. For information, call (213) 222-0546.

To continue the trip, bikers should ride west 1 block on Avenue 43, then turn north on Figueroa Street to Woodside Drive. The Casa de Adobe (5.9) is at 4650 Figueroa Street. This home is actually a replica of an early California hacienda of the period 1800 to 1850. It was built in 1917 by the Hispanic Society of Los Angeles as an example of the secular side of early California life. Visitors may wander through the home, built around a courtyard in the typical style and decorated with period furniture. The home is an adjunct of the Southwest Museum and features a gallery that displays rotating art exhibitions. The Casa is open the same hours as the museum, 11 to 5 Tuesday through Saturday and 1 to 5 Sunday. It is closed Mondays and major holidays.

The ride returns to the park by the same route in reverse, omitting the spur to Heritage Square.

*Note:* While in the area, bikers may wish to visit the Southwest Museum, which houses one of the finest collections of Indian artifacts in the Southwest. Since it is approached by an extremely steep grade, driving there by car is advisable. To reach the museum, drive west on Avenue 43 and north on Figueroa Street. Turn left on Avenue 45, right on Marmion Way and left on Museum Drive. Angle right almost immediately up a steep drive to the museum.

# RIDE 16

# The Kenneth Newell Bikeway

**Distance:** 10 miles round trip

**General Location:** Pasadena

**Features:** One of Los Angeles' first bike trails, this path follows city streets marked with Bike Route signs. Opened in 1966, it was named for the first president of the Pasadena Kiwanis Club, one of the trail's sponsors. It offers close-up views of some fine old Pasadena homes built in the Craftsman style. The trail descends from the bluffs above to the Arroyo Seco floodplain, most famous as the site of the Rose Bowl. The final leg of the trail makes a steep climb out of the floodplain and eventually crosses the dam at Devils Gate Reservoir, drops into Oak Grove Park and ends at the Jet Propulsion Laboratory.

**Difficulty:** Strenuous. Take this ride on low smog days. There is a 320 foot elevation gain, floodplain to Jet Propulsion Laboratory.

**Getting There:** From the Pasadena Freeway (Highway 11) exit north on Orange Grove Avenue. Turn west on Madeline Drive. Stay on Madeline to its 3-point intersection with Grand Avenue and Arroyo Boulevard. Turn south on Arroyo. At the next Y, continue on Arroyo by turning left and uphill. Park on the shoulder off Arroyo just past Columbia Street, which marks the boundary between Pasadena and South Pasadena.

**Finding the Trail:** The trail begins on Arroyo at the city boundary. Ride north on Arroyo, watching for Bike Trail signs.

**Description:** The trail stays on Arroyo past Madeline, then turns right at a Y where Grand again intersects Arroyo. Ride north on Grand, then turn west on California Boulevard for a nice downhill run to California Terrace, where the trail again turns north. In this area are many of Pasadena's finest older homes. This section of the arroyo was settled by artists and other bohemians in the early 1900s. Many advocated the Craftsman aesthetic movement with its admiration for nature and simplicity. The builders used native materials—stone from the creek bed and wood, especially redwood.

A left at Arbor Street (1.1) returns riders to Arroyo where a short, steep hill descends north toward the floodplain of the Arroyo Seco.

Following the floodplain north, bikers pass pleasant Brookside Park with water, rest rooms and tables. Continuing up the floodplain, the trail soon arrives at

the Rose Bowl, the famous setting for the New Year's Day football game. The Rose Bowl is open to visitors 9 to 4 daily except holidays. Enter through the visitor's gate. A massive flea market is held in the Rose Bowl beginning 9 A.M. the second Sunday of each month.

Leaving the Rose Bowl, riders follow Arroyo Boulevard across Rosemont Avenue (2.9), then climb a steep hill out of the arroyo. The trail continues on Arroyo, staying left at Westgate Street and passing through a well-kept suburban neighborhood.

After crossing the Foothill Freeway, the trail turns west on Weimar Avenue, north on Yucca Lane, then swings north on North Arroyo again. A final turn west on La Canada Verdugo Road leads to the end of the street. Bikers continue by lifting bikes over an entrance barrier and riding across the crest of the Devils Gate Dam on an old service road. The dam, another in the series built by the Los Angeles County Flood Control District, drains 32 square miles. Built in 1920, it has a 4,570 acre storage capacity.

After crossing the dam, the trail descends by an old, unused road to Oak Grove County Park, where riders will find water and rest rooms. A ranger station that serves as headquarters for the Arroyo Seco District is open from 8 to 4:30 Monday through Friday.

The trail continues through the park north onto Oak Grove Drive and ends at the Jet Propulsion Laboratory (JPL). This world famous laboratory, which designed the spacecraft that went to the moon, Mars, Jupiter and Saturn, is currently building the Galileo spacecraft, which is expected to be launched in 1986 and arrive at Jupiter in 1988.

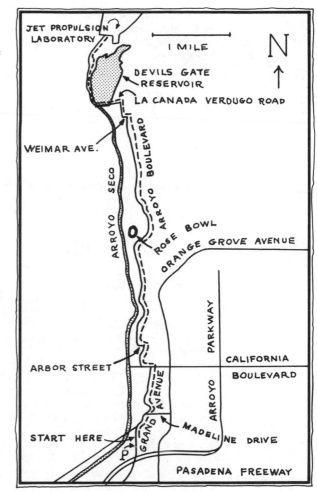

JPL covers 175 acres near the Arroyo Seco and employs nearly 5,000 people.

Guided tours of JPL for groups on weekdays only may be arranged in advance by calling (818) 354-2337. Single riders wishing a tour may arrange to join a group. The tour includes a visit to the assembly facility where spacecraft are being built and to the mission control center, where scientists receive data sent by the probes.

Open house with self-guided tours of JPL, formerly held on the last Sunday of each month, is expected to resume sometime in 1985. The open house has been temporarily discontinued because of construction at the lab.

The return ride is by the same trail in reverse.

# GRIFFITH PARK

Griffith Park is a big park in a big city; it is, in fact, the largest park in a city anywhere in the United States. Sheltered within a bend of the Los Angeles River as it leaves the San Fernando Valley and heads south to the Pacific, Griffith spreads across the eastern end of the Hollywood Hills. Most of its 4,000 acres is wilderness, crossed only by hiking and horse trails; but the landscaped fringes of the park—on much more level ground—have been developed with some of the city's most popular attractions, including 14 miles of bike routes.

The park was originally part of the 6,600 acre Rancho Los Feliz, one of the original Spanish land grants. It was deeded to Vicente Feliz in 1795 by the Spanish crown; it passed to Maria Ygnacia Verdugo in 1843, and 4,071 acres of the holdings were purchased by Colonel Griffith J. Griffith in 1882.

Col. Griffith sold his water rights to the City of Los Angeles two years later, in 1884, for $25,000; and in 1896 he donated 3,015 acres to the city. Over the years he donated another 24 acres and sold the city 353 acres for $143,910, or $407 an acre. The park lost most of its river frontage when the State of California ran the Golden State and Ventura freeways across the northern and eastern boundaries of the park. That loss and other purchases bring the total park area to 4,043 acres.

In his will, Col. Griffith left three-quarters of a million dollars for cultural and civic additions to the park. From these funds the Greek Theatre was built in 1930 and the Griffith Observatory and Planetarium in 1935. Other attractions in the park include golf courses, tennis courts, a swimming pool, merry-go-round, miniature train rides, pony rides, a museum of old trains, fire trucks and cars, and the Los Angeles Zoo. Most of these attractions are adjacent to the bicycle tours described in the section.

The two tours are:

**Ride 17.** Crystal Springs Loop, a moderate 8.3 mile ride from the southern boundary of the park through beautifully landscaped and shaded areas to Travel Town.

**Ride 18.** Mineral Wells Loop, a strenuous loop of slightly shorter length, 7.6 miles, that traverses the Hollywood Hills, then returns along the flat edge of the park.

# RIDE 17

## GRIFFITH PARK

# Crystal Springs Loop

**Distance:** 6.1 miles round trip, Travel Town Loop 8.3 miles round trip including Los Feliz Loop

**General Location:** Los Angeles

**Features:** Following Crystal Springs Road and Zoo Drive, this pleasant bike route passes through shaded eucalyptus groves and the beautifully landscaped flatlands at the eastern edge of Griffith Park. Grassy picnic grounds offer comfortable rest stops, and the merry-go-round and Travel Town provide entertainment at each end of the ride.

**Difficulty:** Easy

**Getting There:** From the Golden State Freeway (I-5), exit west on Los Feliz Boulevard. Turn north into Griffith Park at Crystal Springs Drive and continue on the one-way street 1.1 miles to the visitors center. Turn west to free parking for the merry-go-round.

**Finding the Trail:** The bicycle route is two marked lanes on Cyrstal Springs Drive, one on each side of the road. Descend the steep hill from the parking lot and ride north on Crystal Springs.

**Description:** The ride begins the lazy biker's way: coasting .4 mile downhill to Crystal Springs Road. Although the street's name conjures up images of crystalline water flowing from a mossy spring, don't look for it. Rangers say there never was a spring: the name just sounded good. Across Cyrstal Springs is an original adobe of the Rancho Los Feliz now used as a small nature museum featuring exhibits indigenous to the area. Advance arrangements to visit the museum, which is usually closed, must be made by calling the visitors center at (213) 665-5188. Directly behind the adobe, the stark white minimalist architecture of the park headquarters and visitors center—so minimalist it's difficult to find the entrance—contrasts with the old adobe. In the visitors center, a ranger on duty answers questions and provides visitors with a park map. Water and rest rooms are available at the headquarters.

Towering eucalyptus trees shade Crystal Springs, and the wooded landscape recalls secluded pastoral scenes. Riding north on Crystal Springs, bikers pass the Wilson and Harding golf courses before arriving at the Los Angeles Zoo parking area (1.2). The zoo is well known for its fine animal collection and natural settings. Although a visit to the zoo is usually a day long trip in itself, bikers who wish to stop off for a visit will find the entrance across the pedestrian bridge at the west edge of the parking lot. Entrance tickets are $4.00 for those 16 and over, $1.50 for children 5 to 15 and free for kids under 5. Zoo hours are 10 to 5 in the winter and 10 to 6 in the summer. The zoo is open every day except Christmas.

Returning to the ride, bikers follow the bike trail east as it circumvents the parking lot on a one-way peripheral road. At the northwest corner of the parking lot, a Bike Trail sign indicates two branches. Our ride turns north onto Zoo Drive (1.9). Rising gradually along

a gentle slope, the trail follows Zoo Drive past several pleasant picnic areas to Travel Town (3.2).

Travel Town houses a fine collection of old locomotives and train cars—all outside—as well as a museum full of old fire engines and unique antique cars, such as a 1927 Hupmobile and a 1918 Mack truck. Among the many exhibits visitors will see a 1908 saddle-tank locomotive used in Hawaii to haul sugar cane from plantations to processing mills. During World War II, it carried commuters from Honolulu to Pearl Harbor; and from 1955 to 1961 it operated in Travel Town, carrying thousands of park visitors on the "Crystal Springs and Southwestern" line.

Admission to Travel Town is free. Hours are 10 to 4 Monday through Friday and 10 to 5 weekends and holidays. There is no admittance 30 minutes before closing. Train rides, leaving every 15 minutes weekends and holidays, cost $1.25 for adults and 75 cents for children. Groups of 15 or more pay 50 cents each. Call (213) 662-5874 for information. Travel Town also rents out railroad dining cars for catered children's parties. Call (818) 993-5757 for details.

Leaving Travel Town, bikers return to their cars by riding east on Zoo Drive to the zoo parking lot (4.5), then continuing south on the one-way street past the parking lot (4.9) to the visitors center (5.7), where a stiff pedal up the hill leads to the parking lot (6.1).

Bikers wishing a longer ride should not turn into the parking lot but continue south on Griffith Park Drive to the southern boundary of the park at Los Feliz Boulevard (6.8). Griffith Park is a one-way street here; the return ride is made on the one-way Crystal Springs

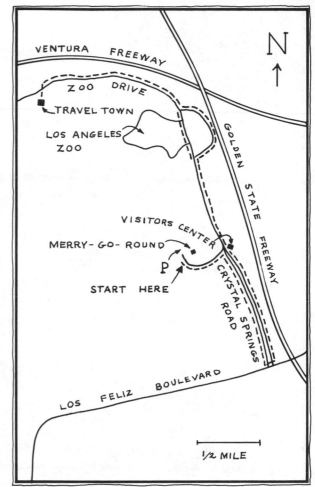

Drive. This loop adds 2.2 miles round trip to the ride and includes a slight grade from Los Feliz to park headquarters.

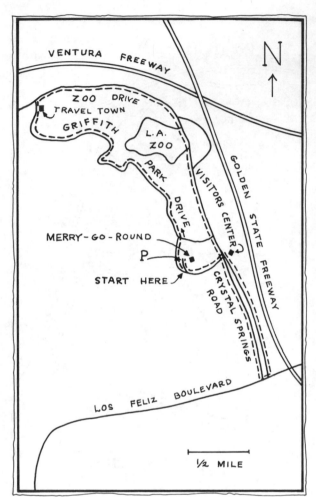

## RIDE 18

### GRIFFITH PARK

# Mineral Wells Loop

**Distance:** 7.6 miles

**General Location:** Los Angeles

**Features:** This short but difficult ride leaves the flatlands of Griffith Park to cross the eastern end of the Hollywood Hills. Pines and chapparal grow on the dry hills, replacing the irrigated landscaping of the lower park. The trip is intended for bikers who are looking for a conditioning workout.

**Difficulty:** Strenuous. Because dumpsters hauling dirt use this road during the week, the ride should only be attempted weekends.

**Elevation Gain:** 160 feet, Crystal Springs Road to Mineral Wells

**Getting There:** Exit the Golden State Freeway (I-5) west on Los Feliz Boulevard and turn north into Griffith Park just beyond the freeway at Crystal Springs Drive. Drive 1.1 miles to the visitors center, then turn west to free parking for the merry-go-round.

**Finding the Trail:** The ride starts uphill at the south end of the parking lot on a road that is blocked off to auto traffic.

**Description:** Gaining elevation, the trail circumvents the large parking lot and north edge of the Cedar Tree picnic grounds; it soon joins Griffith Park Drive, where riders turn north and begin a steady climb past the entrance to the Harding Golf Course clubhouse

and driving range (1.0). The road narrows and begins a steeper climb past the Mineral Wells picnic area, where it reaches its high point, 600 feet, and begins a quick descent to Zoo Drive (2.5).

The ride now picks up the marked bike route on Zoo Drive, turning east past Travel Town and continuing to the first intersection at the zoo parking lot (3.8), where the street temporarily becomes one way. Still a marked bike route, the trail continues south on Crystal Springs Drive past the visitors center (5.0) onto Griffith Park Drive and follows the drive to the south edge of the park at Los Feliz (6.1). Griffith Park Drive is a one-way street during this mile; riders return to the visitors center on the northbound one-way street, Crystal Springs Road (7.2). A short, steep ascent to the parking lot returns riders to their cars (7.6).

Bikers interested in enjoying some of the many park attractions along this route should refer to the Crystal Springs Loop, Ride 17, for details.

## RIDE 19

# Sepulveda Basin Bikeway

**Distance:** 3 miles round trip, West Loop; 5.8 miles round trip, East Loop

**General Location:** Encino

**Features:** Second only in popularity to the South Bay Bicycle Trail, these pleasant, easy loops circle the Sepulveda Dam Recreation Area. The East Loop winds beside a farmer's cornfield, and the West Loop passes the San Fernando Valley Youth Foundation, which, among its many activities, holds weekly bicycle races for young riders through high school age.

**Difficulty:** Easy. The trails are crowded on weekends, and bikers should ride carefully to avoid accidents.

**Getting There:** From the Ventura Freeway (Highway 101), exit north on Balboa Boulevard. Cross Burbank Boulevard and park in the large, free parking area for the Sepulveda Basin Recreation Area on the west side of Balboa just past Burbank.

**Finding the Trail:** The trail runs between the parking lot and the sidewalk paralleling Balboa. Ride the trail to the north end of the parking lot.

**Description:** The two loops of this trail are separated by Balboa Boulevard. Our trip begins by riding the bicycle trail north in a counter-clockwise direction from the parking lot on the West Loop. Cyclists should ignore the first intersection at .3 mile and continue straight ahead. The intersecting trail is the final section of the West Loop and also leads to one of two crossings under Balboa which carry riders to the East Loop.

The trail soon crosses the Los Angeles River on a bridge. By looking down, riders will see the two bike undercrossings, one on each bank of the river. In quick succession the trail passes a second intersection leading to the undercrossing on the north bank of the river, the entrance to the Naval and Marine Corps Reserve Center, where traffic should be watched closely, and the Southern Pacific railroad tracks.

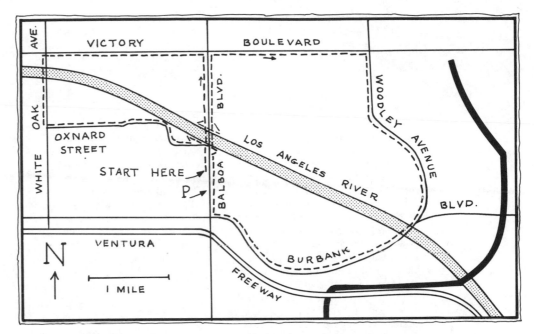

At .8 mile the trail turns west at Victory Boulevard. A large cannon on the lawn to the south marks the site of the California National Guard's 3rd Battalion 144th Field Artillery headquarters (1.3).

Bike races for youngsters four years old through high school teenagers are held on the grounds of the San Fernando Valley Youth Foundation (1.4). Signups and practice start at 6 P.M. Tuesdays and Fridays with races beginning at 7:30 P.M. Sunday signups and practice begin at 2 with races at 3:30. Riders must bring and wear helmets. The races, sanctioned by the American Bicycle Association, are directed by Jimmy Weinert, former world champion motorcycle racer.

The foundation also runs an electric car racing track. The track is open to all families or children who build their own miniature race cars. The cars can be electronically timed on the race track.

San Fernando Valley Youth Foundation, which is run by donations and staffed by volunteers, offers diverse services, including dances, football games for youths and counseling and tutoring programs. For information, call (818) 881-7700.

The trail continues to White Oak Avenue (1.8), crosses the street and continues south on the street to Oxnard Street (2.2). This short segment of the ride is on a marked lane in the street. Still on the street, the trail turns east on Oxnard and soon passes the turnoff to the Encino Velodrome, where Saturday night bicycle races start at 7:30. The bike route again becomes a separate path at 2.7 miles and forks left (the right branch is a skate path). It follows a shaded path through the park to a rest area at 2.9 miles. A brick patio holds a water fountain, benches and bike racks. The trail returns to Balboa and the parking lot (3.0) from the rest area.

Riders who want to take the East Loop leave the path at the rest area and follow the trail junction to the river bank, where the trail drops down the river bank and crosses under Balboa.

The East Loop is longer and has better scenery than its western counterpart. To ride the East Loop clockwise, follow the off-road trail north beside Balboa. Large trees shade the route, which turns east at Victory Boulevard (1.1). After crossing Bull Creek Channel, riders will find a pleasant rest area with brick patio and benches. A second rest area, where Odessa Avenue dead-ends on Victory (1.7), also has a water fountain.

At 2.1 miles the trail turns south at Woodley Avenue. The Woodley Golf Course and a coffee shop are on the right, and across Woodley is an exercise par course and rest rooms.

The large size of the recreation area allows multiple activities. Besides holding three golf courses, tennis courts, the youth foundation and velodrome, land is leased to farmers for growing crops. As bikers ride south on Woodley, they will see cornfields, planted on land that serves as a flood basin during high water.

The buzz and whine of low flying aircraft echoing over the cornstalks indicates bikers are approaching the model airplane field, where model builders gather to fly their radar-directed craft.

At the top of a rise just before the path swings west down the only slope on the trail, is a pleasant tree-shaded table and bench. A stop here offers open views of the Santa Susana Mountains, fields and valley.

The trail parallels Burbank Boulevard as it returns to Balboa. Passing the Encino Municipal Golf Course, the path swings around the north side of the parking lot by the Encino Inn, where there is a coffee shop, rest rooms and a chilled water fountain.

The trail again skirts the north edge of the parking lot, then returns to Balboa, where it continues north to the bridge undercrossing. A return to parking lot (5.8) completes the two loops.

# RIDE 20

# Browns Creek Bikeway

**Distance:** 2.4 miles round trip, Browns Creek Bikeway; 6.5 miles round trip, including loop to Chatsworth Park North and South

**General Location:** Chatsworth

**Features:** The beautiful scenery at the northwestern edge of the San Fernando Valley is well worth exploring by bicycle. The trail runs beside the cemented channel of Browns Creek with splendid views of the irregularly shaped Santa Susana Mountains rising to the west. Leaving the bike trail, the ride follows little used rural streets to extraordinary

Chatsworth Park North. Cupped at the base of an extravagant cliff of sandstone formations, the park is small, intimate and romantically beautiful. The ride returns to Browns Creek Trail through Chatsworth Park South and along one busy four-block stretch of city streets.

**Difficulty:** Easy

**Getting There:** Exit the Ventura Freeway (Highway 101) north on De Soto Avenue. Drive about 5.5 miles and turn west on Lassen Street. Park on Lassen west of Deering Avenue at Browns Creek.

From the Simi Valley Freeway (Highway 118), exit south on De Soto Avenue. Drive about 1.5 miles and turn west on Lassen. Park on Lassen west of Deering Avenue at Browns Creek.

**Finding the Trail:** The trail starts at Lassen Street on the east bank of Browns Creek. Ride north on the trail.

**Description:** After viewing the rusting hulks of cars and trucks abandoned in a small wrecking yard across Browns Creek, bikers leave behind the urban atmosphere with views of the broken outline of the Santa Susana Mountains to the west.

At .6 mile the trail leaves the levee and continues north on the sidewalk a quarter block, where it crosses Devonshire and resumes kitty-cornered along the levee. The path, built of a pleasing tan concrete, passes a pleasant nursery. Opposite the bike route, on the west levee, a horse trail also follows the creek.

The fence that separates the bikeway from adjoining property also serves as rear fence to animal corrals along the way, and youngsters may want to stop and feed a carrot to one of the horses or inspect the goats and cows.

Rest stops with benches and water fountains are available, in quick succession, at Chatsworth Street (0.9) and Variel Avenue (1.0). Large hedges of prickly pear cactus and bright red geraniums line the path as it approaches Rinaldi Street (1.3), where the bikeway ends. (A flood control district gate closes off the path extension to San Fernando Mission Boulevard, .2 mile up the creek.)

Cyclists who only wish to ride the bike path may make the return trip by the same route in reverse from Rinaldi.

Bikers riding the park loop cycle west on Rinaldi to Canoga Avenue (1.8), where a left turn takes them south to Chatsworth (2.1). The route follows Chatsworth west past Topanga Canyon Boulevard (2.6) to the park (3.0).

A thick grove of spreading oaks shades the road as bikers continue west on the park entry road rather than turning into the parking lot. At the road's deadend an angled gate allows cyclists to wheel their bikes through the entry to the beautiful grassy park snuggled at the base of spectacular sandstone cliffs.

Leaving the park, bikers should take the blocked-off road (3.1) just south of the angled gate. A sign on it says, Authorized Vehicles Only. This road circles the western section of the park and finally returns to the parking lot at the corner of Chatsworth and Valley Circle Boulevard (3.5). Exit the parking lot and ride south on Valley Circle Boulevard to Devonshire (3.9). Valley Circle follows the Santa Susana Pass Wash here and is planted with towering banks of flowering oleanders.

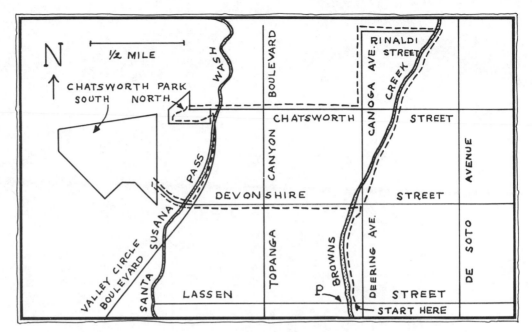

The entrance to Chatsworth Park South is reached by riding west on Devonshire. The south park is larger, more open, and less spectacular than its north counterpart.

A fascinating corner of early Los Angeles is preserved in one corner of the park. The park was originally part of an early Los Angeles homestead. A small section of the homestead has been set aside in the Hill-Palmer Homestead Acre, a Los Angeles historical monument. Open the first Sunday of each month from 1 to 4, the acre includes the early home of Minnie Palmer. Restored by the Chatsworth Historical society, the home is furnished in period furniture. A small museum displays artifacts from the early days of the San Fernando Valley.

After exploring the park, bikers return to Browns Creek Bikeway by riding east on Devonshire past Topanga Canyon Boulevard (5.5) to Canoga Avenue (5.6). There are four blocks of heavy traffic here, and bikers should ride carefully. At Canoga, a right turn leads cyclists to the bike path, where they ride south to Lassen (6.5).

# BIKE LOG

# III

# The Coast

*Once this rocky coast beneath me was a plain of sand; then the sea rose and found a new shoreline. And again in some shadowy future the surf will have ground these rocks to sand and will have returned the coast to its earlier state. And so in my mind's eye these coastal forms merge and blend in shifting, kaleidoscopic pattern in which there is no finality, no ultimate and fixed reality—the earth becoming fluid as the sea itself.*

—RACHEL CARSON
  *The Edge of the Sea*

The curving Los Angeles coastline—from Leo Carrillo State Beach to the San Gabriel River outlet—is an 80 mile stretch of spectacular scenery, and near it are many of the county's most popular bicycle trails. The South Bay Bicycle Trail, best known, most used, runs along 19 miles of shoreline. Nestled near the coast, a series of bike trails circle city and county parks, follow creeks, and pass through quaint seaside communities.

One of the particular pleasures of these trails is that all but one of them can be ridden comfortably at any time of year. Smog along the coast is rarely heavy enough to deter bicycling, and the coast maintains moderate temperatures throughout the year. (The one exception is the Harbor Regional Park ride. The park is situated on the leeward side of the Palos Verdes Hills and escapes neither the inland heat nor contamination on heavy smog days.)

The 11 coastal rides are:

**Rides 21, 22, 23, and 24.** South Bay Bicycle Trail. Four rides on the beach from Santa Monica to Redondo Beach.

**Ride 25.** Santa Monica Loop. An easy ride along beautiful San Vicente Boulevard and the Santa Monica bluffs overlooking the Pacific Ocean.

**Ride 26.** Ballona Creek Bikeway. An easy ride from Marina del Rey along Ballona Creek.

**Ride 27.** Palos Verdes Peninsula Coastline. A moderate ride along the spectacular bluffs of Palos Verdes.

**Ride 28.** Harbor Regional Park. A short but difficult conditioning ride up the Palos Verdes Hills.

**Ride 29.** Shoreline Park. A delightful, easy ride for families through one of the county's best parks.

**Ride 30.** El Dorado Park. A short ride through a beautiful, wooded park around three lakes.

**Ride 31.** Naples. A ride on winding streets to explore the quaint island community of Naples with its immaculate gardens.

# SOUTH BAY BICYCLE TRAIL

The South Bay Bicycle Trail runs 19.1 miles along some of Southern California's most beautiful and well used coastal beaches. It is deservedly the most popular (and most crowded) bike path in Los Angeles County. Riders see exhilarating views of the Pacific Ocean, fleets of weekend sailors, and, on a clear day, Catalina Island riding on the horizon. Bikers may visit five piers and ride through Southern California's largest marina as well as take a Sunday stroll on the Venice boardwalk, the quintessential Southern California experience. Here, the Mad Hatter doffed his top hat, and everything that fell out went for a promenade; everyone else in Los Angeles came to see it.

By December 1985, a mile and a half extension of the trail, north from California Avenue to Chautauqua Boulevard, is scheduled for completion. The trail addition will give riders an uninterrupted 21 mile ride along the Los Angeles shoreline.

The trail has been divided into four rides, each with its specific atmosphere and attractions. One ride is suitable for families with small children; experienced riders may wish to ride the entire trail in one day (38.2 miles round trip).

The four rides are:

**Ride 21.** Santa Monica Pier to Venice Pier. A short ride along the most crowded segment of bicycle path in Los Angeles.

**Ride 22.** Venice Pier to Playa del Rey. A short ride through the Marina del Rey boatyards to the main channel entering the harbor.

**Ride 23.** Playa del Rey to Hermosa Beach Pier. A moderate ride along the beaches in Playa del Rey and Hermosa Beach.

**Ride 24.** Hermosa Beach Pier to Trail's End. A short ride through Redondo Beach with a stop at King Harbor.

# RIDE 21

## SOUTH BAY BICYCLE TRAIL

# Santa Monica Pier to Venice Pier

**Distance:** 7 miles round trip

**General Location:** Santa Monica, Venice

**Features:** Wide open views of the Pacific Ocean to the south and exuberant beach jugglers, musicians, peddlers and strollers on the Venice walkway make this segment of the South Bay Bicycle Trail the most popular in Los Angeles. It is a place where you must join in the fun and smile cheerfully as roller skaters, pedestrians, baby strollers, an occasional bag lady, dogs and joggers obstruct what is supposed to be a separate bikeway.

**Difficulty:** Easy. Suitable for families with small children. Bikers should ride carefully to avoid collisions with others on the path.

**Getting There:** Take the Santa Monica Freeway (I-10) west to its end. Drive north on Pacific Coast Highway. For paid parking, turn left into the first public beach parking lot (about 1 block) after exiting the freeway. Parking is $3 summer, $2 winter.

For free parking, there are two choices. Exit the Santa Monica Freeway at the Fourth and Fifth Street exit. Drive north on Fifth Street; turn left on Broadway, right on Second Street. Park in one of the city parking structures between Broadway and Arizona avenues. Three hours free parking; no validation.

If the parking structures are full, ride west on Arizona to Ocean Avenue. Ride north about 1 mile to San Vicente. Park on San Vicente or one of the side streets in the area.

**Finding the Trail:** The trail begins .3 mile north of the Santa Monica Pier at the north end of the paid parking lot on the beach opposite California Street.

From the city parking structures, ride west 1 block to Ocean Avenue. Ride the bike route on Ocean south to Colorado Boulevard and turn right onto Santa Monica Pier. Take the ramp which leads down under the pier. Ride north .1 mile around the parking lot on the north side of the pier to join the bike path, which passes under the pier here.

From San Vicente, ride south to Ocean. Ride south on the bike route to Colorado and follow instructions above.

**Description:** A loop marking the trail's beginning is equipped with bike racks, benches and a water fountain. After a short ride beside a broad, sandy beach, the trail arrives at the Santa Monica Pier. Although much of the pier was batttered down in the winter storms of '82-'83, some restaurants and attractions remain, including the famous merry-go-round, installed in a roofed enclosure on the pier. Open 10 to 5 Tuesday through Sunday, the merry-go-round was carved in 1922 and installed at its present location in 1947. Restored in 1981, its brightly painted animals will delight children and adults alike. Tickets to ride are 25 cents, and children under 5 must be accompanied by an adult.

To ride up onto the pier, turn off the bike path before it crosses under the pier. Leave the bikeway at the point where a wooden boardwalk crosses the sand and ride toward the pier on the peripheral road bounding the parking lot. Pass the entrance kiosk to the lot. At the stop sign turn right; ride under the pier and go up the wooden ramp leading to the pier. Big Dan's Muscle In Cafe, which over the years has been patronized by assorted celebrities, is just south of the pier on the pedestrian walkway.

Returning to the bike path, our ride continues south through the extensive pilings supporting the various structures attached to the pier and emerges onto broad Santa Monica Beach. At .8 mile the trail, now divided from the pedestrian walkway by a raised curb, runs between another extensive parking lot and the beach. At Navy Street (1.7) it crosses the boundary between Santa Monica and Venice and turns sharply west onto the beach.

*Ride carefully.* A series of unmarked curves in the path through this section sends unwary riders skidding into the sand after they attempt to take the unexpected corners too fast.

At 2.1 miles a walkway leads to an elevated viewing platform with table, chairs and a wooden shade umbrella. The street scene along the following section of the ride is as much fun as the ride itself. Riders may wish to wheel their bikes along the pedestrian walkway either going or on the return trip.

At 2.6 miles the path arrives at the north end of the Venice pavilion. The east wall of the pavilion sports a fine mural of a modern-day Venus roller skating out of a sea shell.

The bikeway continues around the seaward side of the pavilion, passes the weight lifting area, and finally arrives at the Venice Fishing Pier (3.5). A walk out the pier (walk bikes; riding is forbidden on the pier) provides sweeping views of the Santa Monica and Venice beaches as well as the Santa Monica Mountains to the north and the Palos Verdes peninsula to the south. On a clear day Point Dume can be seen to the north and Catalina Island sits low on the horizon just west of Palos Verdes.

**Linking:** The South Bay Bicycle Trail leaves the beach at the pier and continues east on Washington Street. Bikers may follow it an additional 8.4 miles round trip through Marina del Rey to the jetty bordering the entrance channel to the marina. *See Ride 22.*

The return trip is by the same path in reverse. At Windward (by the pavilion), bikers may wish to wheel their bikes along the pedestrian boardwalk to view the astonishing gathering including musicians, the Venice chain saw juggler, a singing swami on roller skates, sidewalk preachers, hustlers and hawkers.

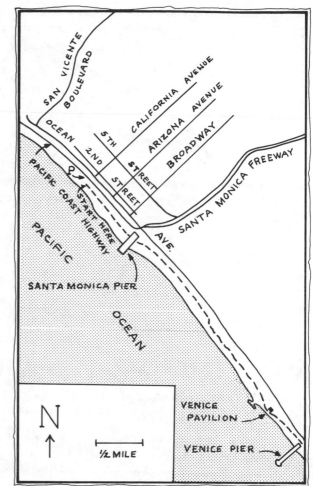

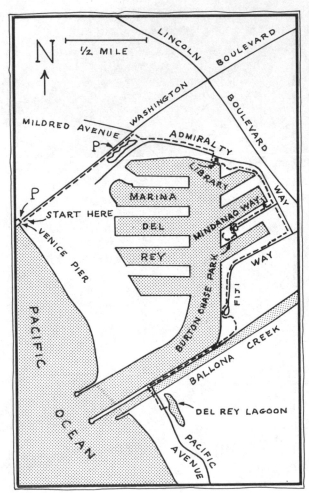

# RIDE 22

## SOUTH BAY BICYCLE TRAIL

# Venice Pier to Playa del Rey

**Distance:** 8.4 miles round trip

**General Location:** Marina del Rey, Playa del Rey

**Features:** Starting from the Venice fishing pier, this trip wends through the Marina del Rey boatyards, offering views of the yachts berthed in the marina. The ride continues to Fisherman's Village, one of the Southland's quaint attempts to recreate an eastern seacoast fishing village. Its quick food stands and 162 hanging bike rack hooks offer riders a relaxing interlude. The main channel leading to the marina, busy with catamarans, yachts, sailboats and motor launches leaving or entering port is a fascinating sight. The end of the jetty is usually full of bikers who have stopped to view the parade. The ride ends at Del Rey Lagoon with its pleasant park and views of neophyte sailors learning to sail.

**Difficulty:** Easy. There is often a headwind blowing inland down the jetty.

**Getting There:** From the Santa Monica Freeway (I-10) exit south on Lincoln Boulevard. Drive 3 miles, then turn west on Washington Boulevard. Continue to the beach parking ($3 summer; $2 winter) at the end of Washington.

From the San Diego Freeway (I-405), exit west on Washington Boulevard and follow the parking instructions above.

For free parking, park on the street near the intersection of Washington and Mildred avenues.

**Finding the Trail:** The trail begins at the foot of the pier. Ride out of the parking lot and continue east on Washington. The trail is a marked route on the street for 8 blocks. Riders parking on Washington should pedal west on Washington to explore the pier, then follow instructions for leaving the parking lot.

**Description:** The ride begins with a sidetrip out Venice pier (walk bikes; riding is forbidden on the pier). On a clear day there are outstanding views of the curving beaches of Santa Monica and Venice as well as of Palos Verdes Peninsula to the south and Point Dume to the north. Catalina Island sits low on the horizon just west of Palos Verdes.

From the pier riders travel east on Washington through a confusing glut of cars backing out of diagonal parking and making U-turns at the end of Washington. These eight blocks are one of the few sections where the 19 mile Beach Bikeway utilizes city streets rather than a separated path.

Marina del Rey, which now houses the largest man-made marina in the United States, is built upon the former wetlands spreading around the outlet of Ballona Creek. One fragment of these marshy areas appears as riders approach the light at Mildred Avenue (0.9). To the right a chain link fence encloses a narrow pond set aside for migratory birds and local waterfowl. It has become a favorite place for local residents to abandon pet ducks and chickens.

Youngsters on the ride will appreciate having a few slices of stale bread to feed to the flock of quacking ducks.

At Mildred the trail turns sharply right, leaving Washington, and proceeds through a pleasant, narrow park bordering Admiralty Way. A par course has been laid out beside the bike trail. The trail crosses Admiralty (1.6), where riders may stop at the Marina library, a branch of the county library system (bike racks; water). It holds an excellent collection of books on sailing and water sports in general.

A sharp turn through narrowly spaced posts at the base of the library parking lot leads riders east along the edge of the marina boat docks with views of row upon row of smartly turned out yachts—more than 10,000 of them—floating documentation of the wealth in Los Angeles. The bikeway, marked by painted stripes, continues through the marina boatyards, then crosses Bali Way (1.8).

At the next street, Mindanao Way (2.0) our ride leaves the bike path proper for a short side trip to the Burton Chase Park bike path. Ride west on Mindanao, circle the U where it deadends and turn into the parking lot for the park. The bike trail leaves from the southwest corner of the parking lot and runs beside Basin H of the marina, where visiting yachts may dock temporarily. This park, with grassy knolls and an elevated viewing platform, affords excellent views of Chace Harbor. The bike path circles around the park, then returns by the same route. Retracing our route on Mindanao, we turn south on the bike path and soon approach the marina visitor's center, where riders may pick up maps and brochures about the area. The trail continues around the marina. At Fiji

Way (2.5) the bikeway turns south and soon leaves a separated path to continue on Fiji south to Fisherman's Village (3.0).

With its cobblestone quay and imitation Cape Cod shops, the village provides an entertaining stop along the route. A walk along the quay gives views of the large yachts which often dock there. Harbor tours depart on the hour every hour from 11 to 5 on the Marina Belle. Adults, $4; children 6–12, $3; and youngsters, $2. Lock bikes securely if you leave them.

Leaving the village, the trail continues on Fiji, makes a U-turn at the street's deadend, then turns immediately south on a marked bike trail entrance (3.3).

**Linking:** A half block beyond Fiji, at Ballona Creek, the trail forks. The east branch, with access through an entrance barrier, follows the north levee of Ballona Creek to Culver City Park. *See Ride 26.*

Our ride turns west out the jetty separating Ballona Creek from the main entrance channel to Marina del Rey. Sailboats tack across the channel out to sea while motor launches chug along the edges of the channel, providing a scene of graceful motion and beauty as shafts of sunlight glance across the sails and gusts of wind riffle them. Bikers and pedestrians stop along the length of the jetty to view the scene. At the north end of the bridge crossing Ballona Creek (4.0), a gate allows entry to the South Jetty Viewing Pier. This viewing point has become a stopping place for bikers for friendly conversations and exchange of information.

Our ride proceeds across the bridge and continues straight south on Pacific Avenue, leaving the bike path, which swings south to the beach just beyond the bridge. The trip ends at the Del Rey Lagoon Park (4.2) four blocks beyond Ballona Creek. The lagoon is the training site for L.A. city recreation classes in sailing and canoeing, and bikers there during classtime may see neophyte sailors learning the ropes or canoeists paddling a slalom course marked out by bobbing buoys.

**Linking:** Bikers may add a 16 mile round trip loop to their ride by continuing south on the South Bay Bicycle Trail to the Hermosa Beach Pier. *See Ride 23.*

Our ride returns following the same route in reverse.

# RIDE 23

## SOUTH BAY BICYCLE TRAIL

# Playa del Rey to Hermosa Beach Pier

**Distance:** 16 miles round trip

**General Location:** Playa del Rey, El Segundo, Manhattan Beach, Hermosa Beach

**Features:** The broad, open expanses of the Playa del Rey beach and a bike path unencumbered by pedestrians make this ride ideal for bikers who simply like to

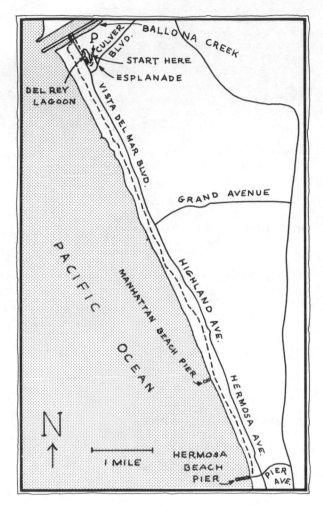

get on their bikes and go. Planes leaving Los Angeles International Airport fly so low over the bike path you want to duck; and hang gliders use these same bluffs for practice flights. On any weekend riders will see the graceful gliders floating silently overhead.

**Difficulty:** Easy. Afternoon headwinds from the north can make the return trip difficult.

**Getting There:** From the end of the Marina Freeway (Highway 90) turn southwest on Culver Boulevard. Drive 2 miles and turn right on Esplanade. Drive 2 blocks and park at Del Rey Lagoon. There is very little parking in Playa del Rey. A second free parking area may be found by continuing 3 blocks southwest past Esplanade on Culver, jogging at Pacific Avenue, then turning south on Trolley Way. Drive to the end of Trolley, turn east on Surf Street, drive one block and turn north on the alley. Park on the cement strip between the alley and Vista del Mar. For a third parking area, turn south on Vista del Mar from Culver, drive up the hill and park on Waterview Street. A steep asphalted trail leads to the beach from the west side of Vista del Mar. Carry bikes about 10 feet across the sand to the bike path.

**Finding the Trail:** Ride north along the west side of the lagoon on Pacific to the footbridge over Ballona Creek. From the alley parking return north on Trolley to Pacific. Ride north on Pacific to the bridge.

**Description:** The trip begins by riding north across the Ballona Creek footbridge for a view of the main channel to the Marina del Rey harbor with its constant flow of boats to and from the Pacific. Recrossing the bridge, we pick up the bike trail as it swings abruptly west just past the south end of the bridge (.2). The Playa del Rey beach lacks public parking and for 2 miles is the broadest and most deserted stretch of sand in Los Angeles County. The

cement bike path curves through the middle of the sand; the ride is swift, unobstructed. Rest rooms, showers and bike racks are spread along the beach. Hang glider pilots use the bluffs flanking the beach for a launch pad, and bikers can watch the colorful gliders float on the air currents above. The bikeway is in the direct path of the big jets leaving nearby LAX; the desolate sand dunes beyond the bluff once housed a neighborhood in Westchester that was torn down to create a sound buffer for the new jet takeoff pattern at the airport. The thunder of the engines is overwhelming if you happen to be under one of these jets as they dust the bluffs above you and rattle the ground underfoot.

We pass the Hyperion Sewage Treatment Plant, the Scattergood Generation Station with its two looming candy striped stacks, and Southern California Edison's El Segundo Generating Station. Massive chunks of this section of the cement trail were washed out in the winter storms of '82-'83 and caused the trail's closure. An exposed section that swung seaward around the Edison generating station was the final segment to be rebuilt. The trail re-opened in the summer of '84.

Entering Manhattan Beach, the bike trail runs along a low shelf cut away by the ocean along the upper edge of the beach. The elevation gives riders a bird's-eye view of the volleyball games and myriad beach activities below. Beach homes, each different and many of interesting design, line the slope above the bike path and allow riders a closeup view. More good views are available by walking out the Redondo Beach pier (7.2), leaving bicycles locked since they are not allowed on the pier.

A half mile beyond the pier our ride leaves the bike path, which continues straight south onto Strand. We turn west and carry our bikes down 13 steps, then turn south again along a combination bike and walkway. Before walking down the stairs, however, turn around and read the sign pointing straight out to sea. "Salsipuedes," it says, "66 km." *Salsipuedes* means "get out if you can."

Further along signs warn that no horses are allowed on the beach. Our ride continues along the Hermosa Beach shoreline to the city pier (8.0). Pier Avenue, which dead-ends at the pier, has a number of good, inexpensive restaurants; and the Lighthouse, the famous jazz club, is located a half block from the beach on the south side of Pier.

**Linking:** The final segment of the South Bay Bicycle Trail adds a 7.6 mile round trip loop to the beach south of King Harbor in Redondo Beach. To ride it, continue south on the bikeway past the Hermosa Beach Pier.

The return ride is along the same trail in reverse.

**Linking:** From Playa del Rey, a round trip loop of 8.4 miles north on the South Bay Bicycle Trail leads to the Venice Pier. To continue north, ride the trail east on the jetty from the Ballona Creek bridge.

# RIDE 24

## SOUTH BAY BICYCLE TRAIL

# Hermosa Beach Pier to Trail's End

**Distance:** 7.6 miles round trip

**General Location:** Hermosa Beach, Redondo Beach

**Features:** This final, short segment of the South Bay Bicycle Trail gives bikers an easy ride and a chance to enjoy the attractions around the Hermosa Beach Pier and at King Harbor in Redondo Beach. After leaving King Harbor, the bikeway follows a sandy beach and ends at the boundary line between Redondo Beach and Torrance.

**Difficulty:** Easy

**Getting There:** Driving south on the San Diego Freeway (I-405), exit west on Rosecrans Avenue. Drive 1.4 miles and turn south on Sepulveda Boulevard (Highway 1). Drive 2.5 miles and turn west on Pier Avenue. Drive across the railroad tracks, then turn south on Valley Drive at the civic center complex. Park in the free lot on the east side of the street. The entrance is marked with a Public Parking sign.

Driving north on the San Diego Freeway (I-405), exit west on Artesia Boulevard. Drive about 3 miles and turn south on Pacific Coast Highway. Drive about a half mile, turn west on Pier Avenue and follow instructions above.

Cycling from this free parking lot, which has a 12-hour time limit, to the South Bay Bicycle Trail adds 1 mile,

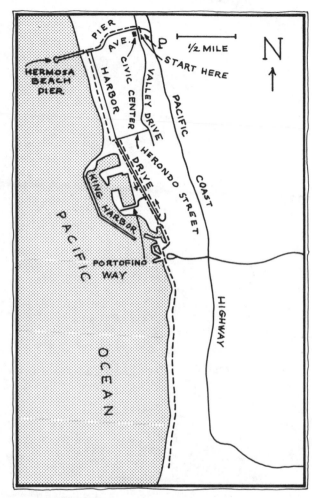

round trip, to the ride. Metered parking with a 2-hour limit is available along Pier toward the beach. The metered parking is free and without time limit on Sunday but is usually full. There are no beach parking areas in the vicinity.

**Finding the Trail:** Ride west on Pier Avenue to the beach. The bikeway here shares the cement promenade along the beach with pedestrians and roller skaters. Ride south on the promenade.

**Description:** A stroll to the end of Hermosa Beach Pier is a pleasant way to begin this ride. Lock bikes or walk them with you as riding is not allowed on the pier. From the end of the pier the sweep of the coastline looks like a large bowl laid on its side with Point Dume to the north one lip, Palos Verdes Peninsula to the south the opposite lip, with the pier sliding down one slope of the bowl. The ocean north of the pier is popular with surfers, and the pier offers a good vantage point to watch them riding the waves.

Returning to the promenade, we turn south and pedal along the beach. The trail becomes progressively less crowded as it proceeds away from the pier. At .7 mile the trail turns abruptly east and leaves the beach. At Harbor Drive and Herondo Street (1 block), the trail becomes a bike route going south on a marked lane on Harbor.

A small rest area at Portofino Way and Harbor (1.2) has bike racks and benches. A sign on the sidewalk beside the rest area guides bikers onto the sidewalk, where they continue south to the Redondo Beach Marina parking area. A former construction job had bikers detouring through the parking lot, and the yellow arrow guiding riders into the lot is still there. *Do not enter the lot.* The construction is completed, and the trail continues south on the sidewalk.

No sign marks the point where bikers leave the sidewalk and enter King Harbor. At the curve in Harbor Drive (1.6), bikers should leave the sidewalk

and continue straight past Captain Kidd's Restaurant to a large brick terrace. After crossing the terrace, a Bike Path sign guides bikers beside a garage structure with the harbor on the right. The boardwalk below the terrace is invisible from the bike path, but it is well worth a visit. Carry bikes down a staircase to get there. Called the International Boardwalk, it houses many small restaurants and snack stands featuring food from all over the world: Vietnamese, Thai, Chinese and Mexican included.

At 1.6 miles the trail swings west and enters a large parking structure. It is the only bike trail I have ever ridden that utilizes a parking structure to move bikers through a crowded area. As the trail emerges from the parking structure (1.8), a red sign warns bikers to Walk Bike. The trail is entering the bustling, popular King Harbor Pier with its myriad shops, restaurants and snack stands. Exploring the pier is a not-to-be-missed side trip.

To continue on the bikeway, wheel bikes east away from the pier; before going up a cement ramp that leads to the road, turn south. Almost immediately a sign states: Resume Riding. A 2 mile ride along the south end of the beach brings bikers to the rather nondescript end of the trail amidst several maintenance buildings.

**Linking:** Conditioned riders may wish to continue to Palos Verdes Peninsula, where a moderate ride of 14.2 miles round trip or a difficult ride of 15.7 miles round trip may be taken. *See Ride 27 and Ride 28.* To reach Malaga Cove Plaza, where the rides begin, ride up the road at the end of the bikeway to the parking lot. Exit the parking lot and

ride south on Paseo de la Playa to its intersection with Palos Verdes Boulevard. Ride south on Palos Verdes Boulevard to the large three-way intersection. Turn sharply right onto Palos Verdes Drive West, then turn left almost immediately into Malaga Cove Plaza (1.1).

The return trip to Hermosa Beach Pier is by the same route in reverse. One deviation is necessary. Leaving the King Harbor complex, bikers should cross Harbor Drive and ride north on the east side of the street. At Beryl Street a sign directs riders onto the sidewalk. Continue on the sidewalk to Herondo Street, where bikers should cross to enter the South Bay Bicycle Trail.

**Linking:** From the pier bikers may continue north on the bikeway to Playa del Rey for an additional 16 miles round trip. *See Ride 23.*

# RIDE 25

# Santa Monica Loop

**Distance:** 10 miles round trip

**General Location:** Santa Monica

**Features:** This ride begins on the bluffs overlooking the Pacific Ocean and follows San Vicente Boulevard with its famous spreading coral trees to the Brentwood Country Mart. Returning to the ocean, it follows the Palisades south to Santa Monica Beach. After a stop to visit Santa Monica Pier, the ride returns to San Vicente along Ocean Avenue. The City of Santa Monica has done an excellent job of developing bike lanes in the bustling seaside area. Bikers are divided from traffic by a painted bike lane along most of this route, including a 2 mile stretch beside the popular Palisades Park.

**Difficulty:** Easy. The route follows a gentle uphill slope along San Vicente. One short, steep hill returns bikers to the Palisades from Santa Monica Beach.

**Getting There:** Exit the Santa Monica Freeway (I-10) at the Fourth and Fifth Street offramp. Drive north on Fourth Street about 1.2 miles and turn west on San Vicente. Park on San Vicente where it ends at Ocean Avenue on the Palisades above the Pacific Ocean.

**Finding the Trail:** The ride begins east on San Vicente Boulevard.

**Description:** The ride up San Vicente to 26th Street follows the most famous jogging route in West Los Angeles. The broad, grassy median strip down the center of San Vicente with its giant coral trees has a dirt path worn bare by the feet of countless joggers. San Vicente is lined with the elegant homes of wealthy Angelenos and is one of the most beautiful streets in Los Angeles.

At 26th Street (2.1) the route turns south, and bikers will see the barn red Brentwood Country Mart, a favorite place to stop for a morning café au lait or barbecued chicken lunch. The mart is a series of small shops with a pleasant interior patio filled with tables and surrounded by food stands. One stand offers an interesting assortment of freshly squeezed exotic fruit juices, and another features shish kabab. For chocoholics, a candy store sells tempting crystallized fruit dipped in chocolate.

Following 26th Street two blocks, the route turns west on Carlyle Avenue (2.2), a lovely street shaded with towering, ancient pine trees. This section of the ride is on unmarked city streets. A right turn at 17th Street (2.9) takes bikers to Georgina Avenue (3.0), where the route turns west once again and returns to the Palisades at Ocean Avenue (4.4).

The route turns south on Ocean, following a painted bike lane on the street beside Palisades Park. The street allows spectacular views of the Pacific Ocean. If bikers wish to explore the narrow park itself, they must walk their bicycles.

A fascinating Camera Obscura is located in a park building just north of Wilshire Boulevard. In the darkened upstairs room, a lens device focuses scenes from outside on a circular white surface in the room. The swiveling lens allows a 360-degree view around the building. Ask at the Senior Recreation Center for free admission to the Camera Obscura.

At Pico Boulevard (6.2), the trail turns right on Barnard Way, which cuts into the intersection at an angle slightly south of Pico.

Barnard descends to the beach, and the route follows it to a curve that takes Barnard east to Neilson Way. Our route turns north here onto the South Bay Bicycle Trail, which parallels Barnard at this point (7.0). If bikers continue around the curve they will find themselves at Neilson; they need to turn around and return to the South Bay Bicycle Trail.

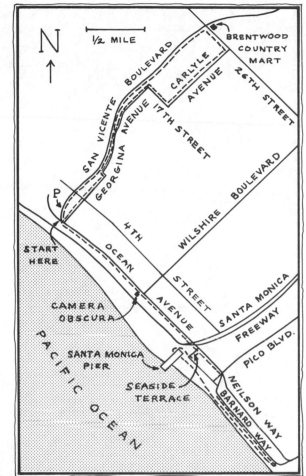

**Linking:** The ride here joins Los Angeles' most popular bike trail, the 19 mile South Bay Bicycle Trail. Cyclists may add a 3 mile round trip loop to this ride by pedaling south on the bikeway to Venice Pier. Further rides lead to Redondo Beach. *See Ride 21.*

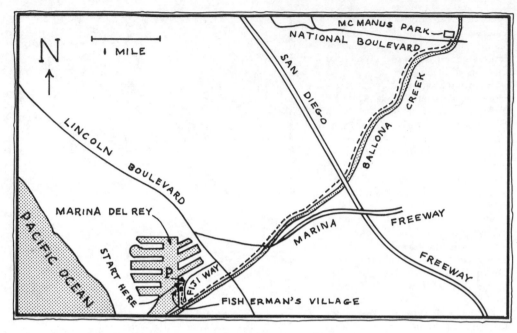

Riding north on the South Bay Bicycle Trail, cyclists soon cross under the Santa Monica Pier. To ride up onto the pier, bikers should turn right on the road skirting the parking lot, then walk up the wooden ramp leading to the pier. After exploring the pier and its famous merry-go-round, bikers should leave the pier on the wooden ramp. Instead of returning to the bikeway, the ride follows the pedestrian walkway south one block to Seaside Terrace (8.2). Walk bikes along this block. A steep climb up Seaside Terrace returns bikers to Ocean Avenue, where the route crosses Ocean and continues north in a painted bike lane, returning to San Vicente at 10 miles.

# RIDE 26
# Ballona Creek Bikeway

**General Location:** Marina del Rey, Culver City

**Distance:** 15.8 miles round trip

**Features:** Riders looking for a way to extend a ride along the South Bay Bicycle Trail like this bikeway. It's uncrowded and has enough ups and downs on street overpasses to exercise one's muscles. As for scenery, it's a bore. A good part of the trail is built halfway down the cement wall that lines what used to be Ballona Creek and the view is of the cement wall along the opposite bank. The trail's unfortunate termina-tion point is a particularly dreary segment of National Boulevard. A pudgy, sulking teenager had the last word on this. Red-faced, she puffed up to the exit and regarded the urban blight surrounding her as I stood by. When her parents arrived, she turned to them accusingly. "This is the worst place you've ever taken me," she said. Actually, there is a small, pleasant park guarded by a chain link fence west of the exit. Bikers willing to negotiate National can ride west, then carry their bikes down a steep set of stairs to enter the park.

**Difficulty:** Easy. Expect afternoon headwinds on the return trip.

**Getting There:** From the end of the Marina Freeway (Highway 90), continue west to Lincoln Boulevard. Turn south on Lincoln, drive 3 long blocks, then turn west on Fiji Way. Take Fiji to Fisherman's Village and park in the free lot there. If it is full, an overflow lot is available between the village and Lincoln.

**Finding the Trail:** Leave the parking lot and ride west on Fiji to its deadend. The bike trail entrance is on the southeast corner of the U-turn at the end of Fiji (0.4). At Ballona Creek our ride forks east along the creek's north levee.

**Description:** Across the flood plain a large LM on the bluffs to the south marks the campus of Loyola Marymount University. Rowing teams from UCLA use the creek for their training, and riders may see the long, narrow boats sprinting along the channel. This beautiful floodplain, one of the last remaining open spaces in West Los Angeles, is soon to be developed. Now used for agriculture, it will eventually look like the rest of Marina del Rey. The trail drops into the creek leveee and crosses under in quick succession: Lincoln Boulevard (1.3), the Marina Freeway (1.9), McConnell Avenue (2.1), Centinela Avenue (2.6), Inglewood Boulevard (2.9), and the San Diego Freeway. There are path entrances at Imlay and Beloit, and the Sepulveda exit (3.8) leads to a McDonald's.

An oddity that could pass for environmental art occurs on the chain link fence separating the trail from the playgrounds of the Culver City junior and senior high schools. A tree evidently grew several branches through the fence links. Nobody noticed these branches as their diameters increased and grew around the links. When crews finally got around to cutting off the branches, they sawed on each side of the fence, leaving round slabs of tree imbedded in the fence and creating a first-rate abstract sculpture.

Weekends the school yard serves as a playing field for lively games of neighborhood soccer. Entire families, from toddlers to grandparents, sit along the grassy slope beside the field and cheer on their team. For those not familiar with soccer, it's a riveting sight to watch an energetic player use his head as a baseball bat.

At Westwood Boulevard and Ocean Drive a footbridge crosses the creek to the school, providing another entry to the bike path.

The ride continues, crossing under Overland Avenue (4.4), Duquesne Avenue, and Higuera Street, and finally exits at National Boulevard (7.9).

A gate in the chain link fence just before National allows riders to enter

McManus Park. If the gate is locked, entry is by riding west on National, then carrying bicycles down a steep staircase. The park, with water, picnic tables, and rest rooms, provides a pleasant break before the return trip.

**Linking:** This trip may be extended by riding the South Bay Bicycle Trip north or south. The south ride continues out the jetty and ends at the Hermosa Beach Pier, adding 16 miles round trip to the ride. *See Ride 23.* The north route begins east on Fiji Way and ends at the Venice Pier, adding 8.4 miles round trip to the ride. *See Ride 22.*

# RIDE 27

## Palos Verdes Peninsula Coastline

**Distance:** 14.2 miles round trip

**General Location:** Palos Verdes Estates and Rancho Palos Verdes

**Features:** Although most of the Palos Verdes peninsula is very hilly, part of the coastal road encircling the peninsula has only moderate slopes. The ride follows this road from Malaga Cove to the magnificent Wayfarers Chapel, affording spectacular views of the Palos Verdes coastline and the Pacific Ocean. The town of Palos Verdes Estates has been gradually building and posting separate bicycle paths and marked lanes

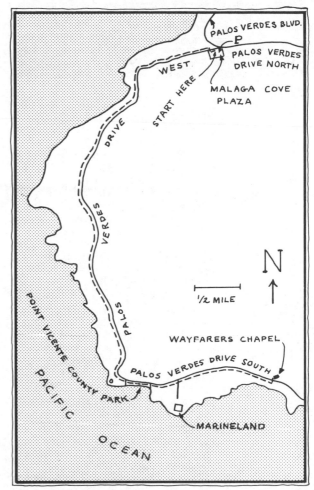

on city streets. Although a short segment of this ride follows a separate bike path, most of the ride is on city streets, some of them with fast moving traffic. Bikes should ride these sections single file with caution.

**Difficulty:** Moderate

**Elevation Gain:** 148 feet

**Getting There:** From the San Diego Freeway (I-405), exit south on Hawthorne Boulevard. Drive 5.7 miles and turn west on Via Valmonte. At Palos Verdes Drive North turn north and follow the road to its intersection with Palos Verdes Boulevard and Palos Verdes Drive West. Stay left onto Palos Verdes Drive West; then turn almost immediately into parking at Malaga Cove Plaza. Parking is marked with 2- and 3-hour limits, not enforced on Sunday. Saturday and weekdays it is best to park on adjacent streets.

**Finding the Trail:** Ride to the west end of Malaga Cove Plaza, then ride west on Palos Verdes Drive West.

**Description:** Leaving Malaga Cove Plaza, where a restaurant and grocery store are available, the route climbs the first grade, a gradual 2 mile ascent to an excellent view of Bluff Cove below. A slumped side road beside Palos Verdes Drive is the first evidence of the unstable ground conditions on the peninsula.

The road soon divides, passing through a pleasant residential area and past a shopping center (2.7). This segment of the ride is fairly level; at Hawthorne Boulevard (4.7), the road dips to Point Vicente County Park (5.5) where bikers will find rest rooms and water. This stopping point offers splendid views of the ocean, the rocky cove below and the Point Vicente lighthouse.

A separate bike path leads from Point Vicente to the Marineland entrance a half mile ahead. The performing killer whales, Orky and Corky, the pilot whale Bubbles, and sea lions and dolphins appear in continuous shows at this famous Southland attraction. Marineland is open from 10 to 5 with the box office closing at 4. Admission is $9.50 adults, $8.00 senior citizens, and $6.85 children ages 3 to 11. Youngsters under 3 are admitted free. Open Wednesday through Sunday during the winter, Marineland stays open all week beginning April 1. A special attraction (costing an extra $4.00) is the swim-through aquarium. Visitors here use swim suits and snorkels provided by Marineland to swim through a tropical aquarium featuring many brightly colored fish. Seeing all the shows at Marineland takes a good four hours so bikers may wish to save this attraction for a separate visit and continue east on Palos Verdes Drive South.

The Wayfarers Chapel, a stunning glass church designed by Lloyd Wright, the son of Frank Lloyd Wright, sits north of Palos Verdes Drive South at 7.1 miles. The graceful, soaring structure is surrounded by beautifully landscaped grounds and is open to the public except when weddings are being held in the chapel. Completed in 1951, the chapel is owned by the Protestant Swedenborgian sect. Tours are offered during the hours 12:30 to 1:30 Friday and Saturday, and movies on Swedenborg and Johnny Appleseed (a Swedenborgian) are also shown. Tours at other times may be arranged in advance by calling (213) 377-1650 or (213) 377-7919.

After touring the chapel, bikers should return to Malaga Cove Plaza by the same route in reverse. It is not advisable for inexperienced bikers to ride further east on Palos Verdes Drive South. Extensive landslides in the Portuguese Bend area just east of the Wayfarer's Chapel have caused the road to be rebuilt to a narrow two lanes with no shoulder.

**Linking:** Bikers looking for a stiff workout can ride east on Palos Verdes Drive North from Malaga Cove Plaza. This bike route, much of it on a separate bike path, leads to Harbor Regional Park. The round trip loop is 13.8 miles. *See Ride 28.*

Bikers may also link with the 19 mile South Bay Bicycle Trail, which follows the coastal beaches. Ride to the three-point intersection from Malaga Cove. Turn north on Palos Verdes Boulevard, then west on Paseo de la Plaza. Enter the beach parking lot at the boundary between Torrance and Redondo Beach. Ride down the steep entrance to the beach. *See Ride 24.*

# RIDE 28

# Harbor Regional Park: A Conditioning Ride

**Distance:** 15.7 miles round trip

**General Location:** Harbor City, Lomita, Rolling Hills Estates

**Features:** The site of a large natural lake, Harbor Regional Park is nestled at the base of the Palos Verdes Hills. One separate bike path leaves the park to make a stiff uphill run to Malaga Cove Plaza 5 miles away. In the park itself a series of all-purpose paths allow bikers to explore the meandering shoreline of the lake. Only the west shoreline is accessible to visitors. A wildlife preserve around the other marshy edges of the lake allows an undisturbed habitat for migratory and resident birds. The scenery is beautiful: stiff clumps of towering rushes grow in the marshes, and thickets of verdant bushes and trees crowd the lakeshore. The ride is an excellent choice for bikers who want to combine a strenuous conditioning ride with a glimpse of undisturbed Southern California marshland.

**Difficulty:** Strenuous

**Elevation Gain:** 463 feet

**Getting There:** From the Harbor Freeway (Highway 11) exit west on Anaheim Street. Drive about 1 mile and turn right into the entrance to Harbor Regional Park. Park in the free lot there.

**Finding the Trail:** There is no separate bike path in the park. Ride through the parking lot to the coral trees marking the entrance to a path leading to the lakeshore. Take that path.

**Description:** By following a series of connecting paths, bikers may explore the park and lake shoreline. Riding to the end of a second parking lot at the north end of the lake allows views of the heavily wooded marshlands around the lake. The round trip for exploring the park is a short 1.9 miles.

To find the entrance to the bike trail starting at the park, bikers should ride toward the south end of the parking lot where they entered the park. The trail leaves from the west edge of the lot near the entrance and is marked with a Bike Trail sign.

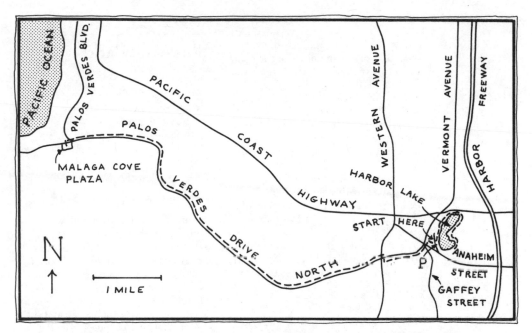

This clearly defined trail passes through an undeveloped area, crosses under Anaheim and emerges at a five-point intersection (0.1) where Anaheim meets Gaffey Street, Vermont Avenue and Palos Verdes Drive North. The trail, which has climbed to be level with Anaheim, then crosses it using the pedestrian crosswalk and continues up the hill on a separate bike path to the left of Palos Verdes Drive North.

At .3 mile the trail passes the entrance to the Los Angeles Youth Hostel. This dormitory style hostelry is open to hardy travelers from all over the world, many who arrive on bicycles. As you puff and pant up the hill, remind yourself of the group of bikers who passed through the hostel several years ago, en route from Alaska to the Queen Mary.

The hostel is on the route of the Pacific Coast Bicentennial Bike Route, which runs from Oregon to Mexico. Flip maps of the route, including accommodations along the way, are on sale at the hostel for $2.95.

The hostel has 65 beds available to members of the International Youth Hostel Federation for $5.25 a night and to non-members for $2.00 extra. Guests share a communal kitchen and may expect to meet visitors from Japan, Australia, New Zealand and Europe, as well as other sections of the United Sections.

The trail proceeds steeply uphill to Western Avenue (0.9), where it crosses to the north side of Palos Verdes Drive North and continues up.

Crossing Palos Verdes Drive East (1.9), the trail continues west up Palos Verdes Drive North through the wooded, rural communities of the peninsula. A grassy square at the intersection of Rolling Hills Road (3.1) offers a welcome rest area with benches, bike racks and a water faucet.

Towering eucalyptus and beautifully landscaped homes line the road as the trail continues on a separate path past Crenshaw Boulevard (3.7). At the three-point intersection of Palos Verdes Drive North with Palos Verdes Boulevard and Palos Verdes Drive West, bikers should stay left to Palos Verdes Drive West. The turn into Malaga Cove Plaza (6.9) is just past the intersection to the left. The plaza has a small grocery store and pleasant outdoor cafe.

**Linking:** Bikers may continue west on Palos Verdes Drive West from Malaga Cove Plaza for a 14.2 mile round trip ride along the bluffs overlooking the Pacific Ocean. *See Ride 27 for details.*

A second route links bikers with the 19 mile South Bay Bicycle Trail, which runs along the coastal beaches. To ride to the bikeway, return to the three-point intersection from Malaga Cove Plaza and turn north on Palos Verdes Boulevard. Turn west on Paseo de la Plaza and enter the beach parking lot at the boundary between Torrance and Redondo Beach. Ride down the steep acess road to the beach. *See Ride 24.*

The return trip is by the same route in reverse.

# RIDE 29

# Shoreline Park

**Distance:** 5.9 miles round trip. Three separate loops allow bikers to ride as little or as much as they wish:
0.7 miles round trip, Lagoon Loop
2.2 miles round trip, Los Angeles River Loop
3 miles round trip, Marina Loop

**General Location:** Long Beach

**Features:** This bike trail follows the Long Beach shoreline from the city beach through the yacht harbor to the Los Angeles River outlet. En route it makes two loops through charming, popular 36-acre Shoreline Park. The park, with its grassy knolls, lagoon, and extensive views of the Pacific and the Queen Mary across Queensway Bay, is one of the most well-liked and well-used parks in the county. The park is crowded on weekends but, strangely enough, not with bikers; the bike trail, the newest in the county, is not well known enough yet. There are excellent barbecue and picnic facilities and one of the best-equipped children's play areas I've seen. Many families bring musical instruments (accordions, guitars, harmonicas) and chairs to settle into and watch the passing boats and strollers.

In Venice, a battle between bikers and roller skaters raged when the bikes-only South Bay Bicycle Trail was first built. A pleasant greeting to a skater on the bike path was a snarled "Get off the bike path." Other comments deteriorated from there. At the battle's pitch, police issued citations to skaters caught on the path.

The Long Beach Shoreline bike paths are a fascinating sociological contrast. The paths take up two-thirds of a wide cement walkway. A dotted line runs down the center of the bike path, but no line separates bikers from the final third of the path, which is occupied by pedestrians, skateboarders, rollers skaters and an occasional bag man, all of whom fan out to occupy the entire path. Riding here on a crowded afternoon is like wending one's way through a crowd of ponderous, migrating water buffalo. But everyone is cheerful. An air of sharing, enjoyment and live-and-let-live pervades the atmosphere and makes any inconvenience easily ignored; and, once the trail leaves the park proper, pedestrians disappear and bikers have free wheeling.

**Difficulty:** Easy. An excellent ride for families.

**Getting There:** Drive south on the Long Beach Freeway (Highway 7). Exits at the end of the freeway are confusing, so follow them in this order: 1. Take the left exit to Downtown Long Beach (*not* right to Port of Long Beach, Terminal Island and Queen Mary). 2. Exit to the Convention Center and Catalina Island. 3. Pass the second Convention Center and Golden Shore exit. 4. Take the Shoreline Park exit. At Pine Avenue turn south and park in any of Shoreline's free parking areas. Commercial parking between Ocean Boulevard and Shoreline Drive is $3. If parking is difficult to find near the beach on weekends, bikers may drive north and find free parking Sunday on one of the north-south streets west of Pine. Weekdays and Saturdays parking in this area is metered for a 2-hour limit.

**Finding the Trail:** Ride south on Pine Avenue until it ends at Shoreline Park. At this point the trail runs parallel to Shoreline Drive on its south side. Ride east on this trail.

**Description, Lagoon Loop:** The marked bike trail that leaves east from the south end of Pine Street peters out in about 100 yards at the base of the viewing platform and overhead walkway to the convention center. If you mistakenly take it, lock the bikes and climb the tower for an overview of the area; then return to Pine, again ride east but veer south on the first unmarked path that descends an embankment and leads to the bridge crossing the lagoon entrance. Cross the bridge. Here is the entrance to two of the trails.

Turn right to follow the .7 mile trail around the 14-acre lagoon. On the knolls above the south shore of the lagoon is the children's play area, full of climbing apparatus, one of which may tempt bikers of all ages off the trail for a trial ride. It is a metal triangle attached to a pulley that slides across a suspended cable. A rope dangles from the triangle. Riders hang onto the triangle, wrap their legs around the rope, and slide across the cable, just like a provincial James Bond. Beyond the play area are picnic tables and barbecue stoves. The top of the knoll affords excellent views of the Queen Mary. The lagoon trail soon returns to the bridge, where riders may fill their water bottles at a fountain.

**Description, Shoreline Loop:** Cross the bridge again. This time, turn left and follow the second trail, which loops around the shoreline to the Los Angeles River. East of the path is the 131-slip Shoreline Harbor Marina, and beyond the marina the Victorian-style Shoreline Village is seen. Stops may be made at

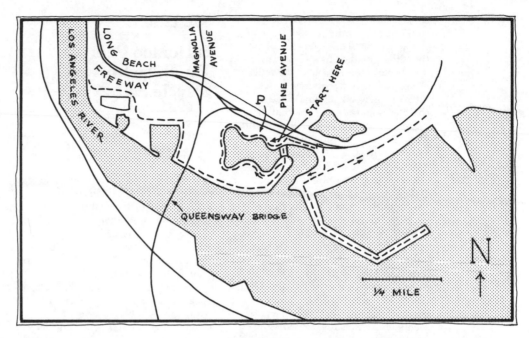

several observation platforms with views of the harbor and the Queen Mary.

The trail turns north (.5) around a small landing basin where visitors catch both the Catalina Island and Long Beach Harbor Cruise boats. The 1½ hour harbor cruise leaves at noon and 2 P.M. both Saturday and Sunday. Bikers who wish to take the ride should be at the landing 30 to 45 minutes before the boat departs. Cost is $6.00 adult and $3.75 children ages 2–11. Information: (213) 514-3838.

The trail leaves the waterfront at the northwest end of the basin and turns right, then left around the large headquarters for the California State University and Colleges. After crossing a large parking area, the trail swings north and

ends at the mouth of the Los Angeles River. The return is by the same trail in reverse.

**Linking:** An open gate in the fence along the river marks the end of the Lario Trail, which follows the Los Angeles River and the Rio Hondo 29.2 miles one-way to the Peck Road Water Conservation Park in El Monte. *See Rides 10, 9, 8, and 7 for detailed descriptions.*

**Description, Marina Loop:** After completing the Shoreline Loop, cross the bridge over the lagoon entrance and return to the bike path paralleling the sidewalk along the parking lot. Take the path east; when it ends at the viewing platform, ride into the street and continue east .1 mile. To the right, wooden stairs lead to the Shoreline Village stores. Here the trail crosses the road to the northeast, then enters a path around the village marked by a black wrought-iron fence. Turning south, the trail crosses an entry to parking for the village, where bikers should keep a sharp eye out for cars. The trail then crosses a street (0.3) leading to marina parking. After crossing the street, the trail branches east and west.

Our ride first turns west, crosses the entrance to the marina parking (0.4), and swings south to follow the entire length of the extended jetty that encloses the marina. Spectacular views of the Queen Mary across broad Queensway Bay and gargantuan oil tankers at anchor in the ocean beyond make this jetty a striking setting for a ride.

At the end of the jetty (1.0), the trail makes a U-turn and follows the inner edge of the jetty, affording views of seemingly endless rows of natty, sparkling white boats docked in the 1,964-slip Downtown Shoreline Marina. Several rest rooms are available along the jetty. Our ride returns to the intersection of the two trail branches (1.7). We continue straight ahead, east, to the city beach (2.1). The bike trail proper turns north here but soon ends in a parking lot. Our ride turns south out the paved jetty that forms the east end of the marina (2.3). Fisher people are perched on rocks along the jetty, and more find views of the ocean, beach and marina are available.

To return, retrace the same path to the intersection (2.6), being sure to turn north around Shoreline Village at the wrought-iron picket fence.

# RIDE 30

# El Dorado Park: The Billie Boswell Bicycle Path

**General Location:** Long Beach

**Distance:** 4.8 miles round trip

**Features:** Gentle, grassy slopes and groves of arching, deciduous trees create a sense of riding through the English countryside rather than the dry California coastline. This park charms ex-Easterners who retain trace memories of green landscapes. The nature trail here, although not devoted solely to native Californian plants, wanders beside an enchanting lake; and the bike trail passes four other lakes as it winds through the park. Like the Whittier Narrows, El Dorado is a natural bottomland, built in the angle formed by the confluence of two rivers, the San Gabriel and Coyote Creek.

**Difficulty:** Very easy. Excellent for families.

**Getting There:** From the San Diego Freeway (I-405), exit north on Palo Verdes Avenue. Drive .9 mile and turn east on Spring Street. Park free on the street just west of the bridge crossing the San Gabriel River, or continue on Spring across the bridge and turn south into the park entrance (parking $2).

From the San Gabriel River Freeway (I-605), exit west on Willow Street (Willow becomes Katella Avenue in Orange County). Turn north on Studebaker Road and east on Spring Street. Follow parking instructions above.

**Finding the Trail:** From the parking lot ride west toward the river levee on the park road that parallels Spring. Continue through the tunnel crossing under Spring. The trail, a combination of park roads and separate paths, turns north on the road paralleling the river levee. *Note:* Spring Street, a divided road, bisects the park, which is completely fenced. There are entrance kiosks on both sides of Spring. If bikers enter the north gate, they should turn west just past the kiosk and follow the road almost to the levee, where the trail turns north.

**Description:** This trail can be confusing because at points it utilizes a separate cement path beside the road, then, for no apparent reason, returns to a park road. The roads, however, have few cars on them, and little harm is done if bikers miss the path and continue on the road.

Our ride begins clockwise on a road paralleling the levee. An archery range is situated to the east of the road, and at .3 mile the trail turns onto a separate path. Shortly before crossing under Wardlow Road in a second tunnel, the trail branches. We proceed through the tunnel, leaving the east loop for the return trip. The trail crosses the road (0.7), then arrives at a second trail junction beside a children's playground. We turn north and follow a separate path in a wide loop around the north end of the park, passing a field where hobbyists fly their radio-controlled gliders, then approach one of the four lakes.

A boat dock renting small paddle boats is located on the southeast corner of the second lake. To get there, turn south on the peripheral road and continue to the second parking lot. The bike trail turns west through the first parking lot and crosses a bridge spanning the stream that joins the upper and lower Milton B. Arthur lakes. The trail again divides. The left fork passes the ranger station and continues around a pleasant, open field. At the road intersection, both trails rejoin, turn west, and return to the trail junction by the playground (2.1).

By again crossing under Wardlow Road, bikers return to the east trail branch passed earlier. This branch, a separate path, makes a loop around the central area of the park, passing through groves of beautiful, mature trees before returning to the entrance kiosk on the north side of Spring (3.4).

Here an optional loop extends the ride a mile. Ride north on the road leaving the kiosk. Stay right to cross a bridge spanning the stream joining the third and fourth lakes; the road then meanders around the lake and loops back to the entrance kiosk.

The path to the nature center leaves from the west edge of the parking lot on the south side of Spring. After locking bikes, riders may wish to explore the center. Two nature trails are open from 8 to 4 Wednesday through Sunday. The museum stays open until 5. The center is closed Monday and Tuesday. The first trail is a mile long and takes 45 minutes. The longer trail adds a second mile and takes 90 minutes.

Jackrabbits, cottontails and red foxes live in the nature preserve, and lucky strollers may catch a glimpse of them. A numbered booklet available free in the museum correlates with numbered stakes along the path and describes the assorted plants and animals visitors are

likely to see. An observation tower allows views of Mount Baldy and Catalina Island on a clear day.

**Linking:** The San Gabriel River Bicycle Trail runs along the levee at the west edge of the park. An additional 10.8 miles round trip takes bikers to the Pacific Ocean (*see Ride 6*), and an additional 16.8 miles round trip heads north to Wilderness Park. *See Ride 5.*

# RIDE 31

## Naples

**Distance:** About 7 miles round trip

**General Location:** Naples, Long Beach

**Features:** This free-form bike ride has no set route but merely gets you to the fascinating island community of Naples and leaves you to explore the tiny community as much as you wish. Marina Park, with swimming and paddle boat rental, is a refreshing location for a rest stop or picnic lunch and affords views of the Marina Pacifica opposite and the entrance to the Marine Stadium to the northwest.

**Difficulty:** Easy. This ride is on city streets and is not advised for small children.

**Getting There:** From the Long Beach Freeway (Highway 7), follow exit signs

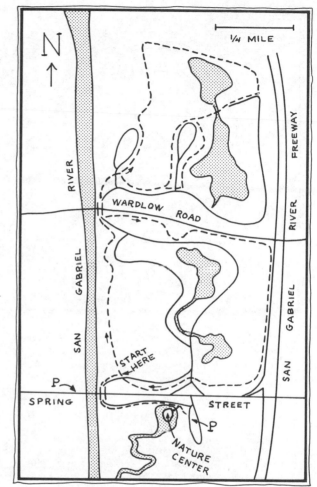

in this order: 1. Take the left exit to Downtown Long Beach. 2. Exit to the Convention Center and Catalina Island. 3. Take the second Convention Center and Golden Shore exit. 4. Turn north on Golden Shore, then turn east on Ocean Boulevard and follow it about 5.3 miles to the mouth of Alamitos Bay.

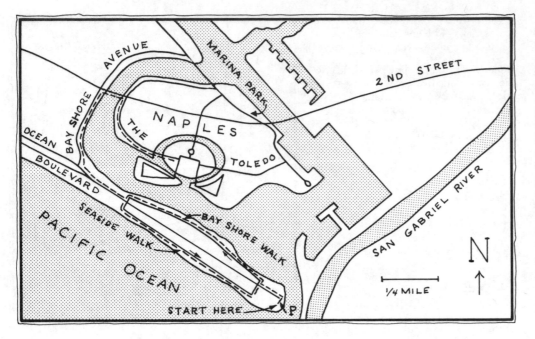

Just before the street swings south, turn left into the free parking lot there. Arrive early weekends when the lot will be crowded.

**Finding the Trail:** There is no bike trail as such. Begin the trip by riding west on Ocean.

**Description:** The long jetty jutting south from the parking lot marks the entrance to Alamitos Bay from the Pacific. This parking lot is situated at the end of the narrow spit of land (a part of Long Beach) that divides Alamitos Bay from the ocena. At 69th Place turn north 1 block to Alamitos Bay and follow Bay Shore Walk north to 55th Place. Ride south 1 block and continue west on Ocean to Bay Shore Avenue, which follows the west side of Alamitos Bay. Turn north on Bay Shore.

Weekends Alamitos Bay Beach along this crowded street is a favorite meeting spot for beach goers.

After wending your way carefully through the slow-moving cars and pedestrians along the street, turn east at Second Street and cross the bridge into Naples.

This small community, which is actually a part of Long Beach, is built on two islands: a large, outer island and a small island within the larger one, surrounded by a channel. The charm of this ride is in discovering the many quaint homes and delightful gardens tucked into this small space. Bikers may wander freely as the islands are so small it is difficult to get lost.

To explore the smaller island, turn south on The Toledo just after exiting the bridge. Follow The Toledo until it crosses the bridge onto the center island. Now you are free to explore as you wish, winding around the curving streets, all only a block or two from Rivo Alto Canal, which surrounds the inner island. Note particularly the well-kept homes, individual architectural styles and charming gardens. At the center of the inner island is a small plaza with a fountain where bikers may stop for a rest.

The Toledo exits the east edge of the inner island on a second bridge. Here bikers may wish to turn south and follow a path around the edge of the outer island. This route will eventually pass the Long Beach Yacht Club, cross under Second Street and arrive at Marina Park, where bikers may have a picnic on the grassy lawn or walk down to the sandy beach for a swim. Paddle boats may be rented here for a trip around the waterfront.

After exploring Naples' outer island, bikers may return to the bridge crossing into Long Beach by following Second Street west. The street has some interesting small restaurants if you are looking for a place to eat.

To return, retrace the same route to 55th Place. Turn south 1 block to the ocean and ride east on Seaside Walk to 69th Street, where a left turn returns you to Ocean. Ride east on Ocean to the parking lot.

# BIKE LOG

# IV

# The California Aqueduct and the High Desert

*The desert says nothing. Completely passive, acted upon but never acting, the desert lies there like the bare skeleton of Being, spare, sparse, austere, utterly worthless, inviting not love but contemplation.*

—EDWARD ABBEY
Desert Solitaire

The high desert of the Antelope Valley is a land of stark, harsh beauty. Coyotes share this unforgiving environment with rattlers and rabbits. The landscape has been painted with an extraordinary pastel brush; pale violets, blues and greens wash the hills. The desert junipers lean southeast, bent by perpetual winds; the primordial Joshua trees stand sentinel, prickly, incomprehensible. Once a year this dormant land blazes briefly with wild, exuberant color after the spring rains bring alive the wild flowers. After the bloom, the land appears desiccated, dead; but those who have come to know the desert return to it again and again. It holds a complex beauty and fascination lacking in any other landscape.

Bikers can explore this unforgiving area with comparative ease because almost a hundred miles of bike trail run through the Antelope Valley. This trail follows the California Aqueduct from Quail Lake near Gorman to Silverwood Lake in the San Bernardino Mountains, a distance of 107 miles. The trail leaves the aqueduct to utilize county roads for only seven miles of its length.

When completed, the California Aqueduct Bikeway will be an imposing monument to non-motorized travel. It is expected to run from the Sacramento Delta to the Tehachapi, where the aqueduct disappears as Northern California's water is pumped through pipes over the mountains. It resumes at Quail Lake, where the aqueduct emerges from the Tehachapi, and stops at Silverwood. The length will be a total of 397 miles.

The first section of the bikeway, opened in 1972, was a 70 mile run in the San Joaquin Valley. The Antelope Valley segment opened a year later in 1973. The bikeway is designed with rest stops (tables and shade ramadas), toilets and parking approximately every 10 miles. Although trail brochures state that water is available at the stops, I found only one water faucet in the segments I rode, and it was broken. It is imperative to carry water, repair tools, snacks, and a sweater on these rides. The desert is shaped by climatic extremes. Riders can wilt under the intense sun, then be bone-chilled as the sun sinks and the winds rise. A flat tire without a repair kit is a disaster: the trail is deserted, and civilization is far away. Elevation in the Antelope Valley is 3,000 feet, and riders will find themselves breathless sooner than at sea level. The headwinds that rise regularly from the northwest are fierce: most intense in the afternoons when riders can find themselves pedaling downhill rather than coasting. Bikers have complained of sand blown by the winds scouring the finish from their bikes, but the rides described here were free of this inconvenience when I rode them.

Because the high desert is untamed and unpredictable, these rides are described as strenuous. If bikers attempt them on a cool, windless day, they will find only the hilly sections to be strenuous. The high desert is a place of such beauty that I hope all bikers will travel there to explore its unique environment, which includes clean air, clear skies and a timeless tranquility.

Three California Aqueduct rides in different areas of the high desert are described here. They are:

**Ride 32.** Quail Lake Loop. This ride circles half of Quail Lake, then follows the aqueduct out of the Tehachapi into the Antelope Valley.

**Ride 33.** The Poppy Pedal. This ride follows little-used Lancaster Road through the California Poppy Preserve, then returns along the aqueduct.

**Ride 34.** Valyermo Loop. Following the aqueduct through the hills above Pearblossom, this ride drops to the valley floor, then regains the aqueduct on Valyermo Road.

These rides explore the aqueduct in the north, central and south areas of the Antelope Valley. For those who wish to see more of the desert, the following table lists entry points to the aqueduct bikeway.

# RIDE 32

# Quail Lake Loop

**Distance:** 23 miles round trip; 18.8 miles round trip on Highway 138 alternate route

**General Location:** Tehachapi Mountains, northern Antelope Valley

**Features:** This ride begins on top of the San Andreas Earthquake Fault at Quail Lake. The northernmost segment of the Antelope Valley aqueduct bikeway, it

| Aqueduct Mileage | Parking Area | Rest Stop | Toilet | Location |
|---|---|---|---|---|
| 1.7 | No | Yes | No | Intersection of aqueduct and Quail Lake service road |
| 11.5 | No | Yes | No | 300th Street West |
| 16.7 | Yes | No | No | Highway 138 |
| 19.7 | No | Yes | Yes | Lancaster Road |
| 28.7 | Yes | No | Yes | Munz Ranch Road |
| 32.7 | Yes | Yes | Yes | 110th Street West |
| 38.0 | Yes | No | Yes | 60th Street West |
| 48.4 | Yes | No | Yes | Avenue S |
| 49.7 | No | Yes | No | Barrel Springs Road at Highway 14 |
| 51.6 | Yes | No | No | Sierra Highway |
| 56.6 | No | Yes | Yes | Cheseboro Road |
| 58.3 | Yes | No | No | Little Rock Siphon fishing access at 82nd Street and Fort Tejon Road |
| 64.4 | Yes | No | Yes | Longview Road |
| 66.9 | No | Yes | Yes | Valyermo Road |
| 73.4 | Yes | No | Yes | Largo Vista |
| 78.3 | No | Yes | Yes | Near Mescal Wildlife Sanctuary |
| 80.5 | Yes | No | No | Oasis Road |
| 85.6 | Yes | No | No | Sheep Creek Road |
| 86.0 | No | Yes | Yes | Johnson Road |
| 96.8 | Yes | No | Yes | Amargosa Road |
| 107.2 | Yes | No | No | Silverwood Lake |

*Note:* Parking for one or two cars on the shoulder of the road is available at most entry points.

circles the north shore of the lake, then follows the aqueduct through beautiful, barren desert hills until it drops into the Antelope Valley to rejoin the aqueduct. The silent, endless flow of the aqueduct contrasted with barren, monotonous reaches of desert make this section of the ride almost mesmerizing. Bikers can easily continue along the aqueduct as far as they wish, but the first valley rest stop marks the turning point for this trip.

**Difficulty:** Strenuous

**Elevation Gain:** 347 feet, valley floor to Quail Lake. There is one very steep hill with a drop of 219 feet at the Oso Pumping Plant.

**Getting There:** Take Interstate 5 north 37 miles from its intersection with the Foothill Freeway (I-210). Exit east on Highway 138 and drive about 3 miles. Look for the Bikeway sign pointing to parking on the north side of the highway.

**Finding the Trail:** The bikeway entry is located at the north end of the parking lot. Ride left of the maintenance station, then turn north.

**Description:** Departing on the service road that loops around Quail Lake, the trail undulates across the steep hills that rise from the lake's north shore. By pausing at one of the view points along the road, bikers may look down on Quail Lake, which was created by the San Andreas Fault. It is one in a series of small lakes—or sag ponds—formed when seismic activity along the fault caused a depression in the ground which later filled with water. Other sag ponds along this section of the fault are Hughes, Munz and Elizabeth lakes.

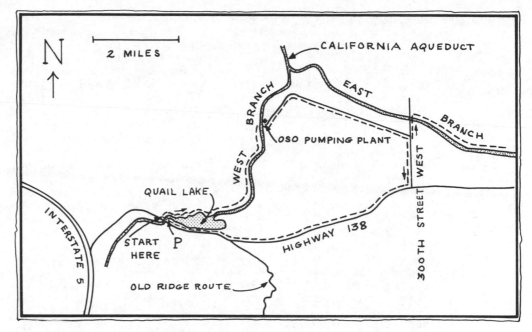

The last time the fault slipped at the lake was more than a hundred years ago, in 1857. A sheep corral next to the lake was shifted from an "O" to an "S" shape, and the sheep were so shook up they scattered across the hills and weren't found for days. Quail Lake was then part of Rancho Tejon, one of the original California land grants from the Spanish crown to settlers. The ranch at the time stretched from Quail Lake to the outskirts of Bakersfield and was owned by Gen. E. F. Beale. Now one of the huge mega-farms profiting from cheap water supplied by the California Aqueduct, the Tejon Ranch is owned in part by the Chandler family, best known as owners of the *Los Angeles Times*.

Engineers designing the California aqueduct were faced with the problem of moving the water safely over the San Andreas Fault. An earthquake along the fault as intense as the one that crumbled San Francisco in 1906 would snap water pipes on the fault like matchsticks and crack apart the cement aqueduct. The natural sag ponds were used to solve the problem. Water from the west branch of the aqueduct flows into the north end of Quail Lake, crosses the rift, and flows out the south end into a continuation of the aqueduct. The water from this branch eventually flows into Pyramid Lake and then Castaic Lake, where it is stored for delivery to Los Angeles and other coastal cities of Southern California.

When the aqueduct was opened, San Joaquin Valley fish somehow managed to migrate through the power and pumping plants to Quail Lake. Fisher people can't carp at finding striped bass, catfish and crappie in the lake.

Before riding on to the aqueduct, bikers may view the extensive damage caused by the rift zone: shattered hills, jumbled ridges and tilted blocks distorted by seismic movement.

A rest stop with tables under a shade ramada marks the intersection of the road with the aqueduct trail (1.7). The bikeway continues on the west bank of the aqueduct 2.8 miles to the Oso Pumping Plant, one of five pumps which lift the Feather River water from Bakersfield over the Tehachapi. North across the valley, aqueduct water flows out of the Carley V. Porter tunnel into the Tehachapi Afterbay, then splits into the east and west branches. The Oso pump lifts the west branch water 180 feet through pipes seen ascending the hill. The bike trail leaves the west branch of the aqueduct here and descends a steep hill on an access road to the pumping plant. Turning northeast, the trail circumvents a fenced hillside range where Brahman bulls, atavistic against the desert hills, watch suspiciously from a safe distance.

Another sharp descent leads to a right turn at the floor of the Antelope Valley (5.6). The road passes through the center of a farm with a pleasant copse of cottonwoods, which riders should particularly enjoy as they are the only trees on this ride. The bike route continues 3.1 miles on the unmarked county road, passing two side roads leading to the aqueduct marked No Bicycles. The trail returns to the aqueduct by turning north on 300th

Street West, marked at the intersection by a Bike Trail sign pointing north. The street itself is not signed. The bike route crosses a bridge over the aqueduct, then turns east down a short, steep incline to follow the aqueduct's north bank (9.0).

The bikeway skirts to the north of a small dam (9.8) and crosses an unmarked road at 11.3 miles, arriving at the rest stop marking the halfway point of this ride (11.5).

The desert appears so vast and barren that riders tend to take special note of any life that appears. I saw a magnificent blue heron, a seasonal migrant through the area, soaring and swooping along the path of the aqueduct. With its white head, black body and six-foot wing spread, the heron is a magnificent sight, its long legs stretched out like a spear in flight. Bikers may also see golden eagles or hawks as well as ducks, geese and coots. Near the lake, blackbirds, wrens, robins and thrashers hop about the brush.

On the return trip, bikers wishing a different, shorter route should continue south on 300th Street West past the turn for the bike path .8 mile to Highway 138, then return to Quail Lake by riding west on the highway. Although it is not a heavily used road, traffic is swift. The ascent to the lake on the highway is more gradual than the abrupt climb to the Oso Pumping Plant on the bikeway.

# RIDE 33
# The Poppy Pedal

**Distance:** 17.9 miles round trip

**General Location:** Antelope Valley

**Features:** Among the most spectacular sights in Southern California are those during the few weeks each year when spring rains bring the desert suddenly alive with a wash of brilliant color: wild flower season. This ride is designed to take advantage of the California Poppy Preserve, a 1700 acre state conservation area of grassland set aside to protect the wild flowers from obliteration by encroaching development. The trip offers sweeping views across Antelope Valley and may be taken at any time of year; but only by choosing a day after the rains may riders experience the desert at its vivid best. The season generally runs from four to six weeks between late March and mid-June, with exact dates dependent on the rain. Riders may call the Poppy Preserve office, (805) 724-1180, for information on wild flower bloom.

**Difficulty:** Strenuous. Prevailing headwinds and three moderate grades increase the stamina needed for the ride.

**Elevation Gain:** 400 feet, floor of Antelope Valley to the California aqueduct

**Getting There:** Take the Golden State Freeway (I-5) north to the Antelope Valley Freeway (Highway 14). Drive 46 miles on 14 and exit west on Avenue I in Lancaster. Turn north after 9.5 miles as Avenue I becomes Lancaster Road. Continue 2 miles; turn south on Munz

Ranch Road. Drive 3 miles and turn east into parking for the California Aqueduct Bikeway.

**Finding the Trail:** The ride begins north down Munz Road Road.

**Description:** Check brakes before starting because this ride begins with an exhilarating 3-mile descent into the Antelope Valley. At Lancaster (2.9) turn west and follow the gently undulating road as it climbs gradually to the poppy preserve. A stiffer grade leads to the entrance road to the Jane S. Pinheiro Interpretative Center (5.3). Unfortunately, the half-mile entrance road, composed of large, unpacked gravel, is not suitable for bicycles. Bikers must lock their bikes and walk in or visit later by car.

The center is open during the flower season 10 to 3 weekdays and 9 to 4 weekends. It features an excellent 7-minute video of the preserve and its spectacular flower displays. Wall graphics show how solar energy powers the building. Hiking trails leave from the center, and rest rooms and water are available.

Continuing on Lancaster, bikers turn north at 160th Street West and soon arrive at the Fairmont Inn (7.0), a roadhouse selling beer, wine, soft drinks, and snacks. The only rest stop on the road, it opens at 11 A.M. daily. The inn is closed Wednesday and Thursday.

The road turns west again, providing striking views of the mountains rising abruptly across the valley. At 190th Street West (10.5) the highway turns north. Our trip ignores the turn and continues straight ahead across a dirt bypass to a short segment of pavement also labeled Lancaster Road. It quickly turns west, becoming 195th Street West. Now the road begins a slow,

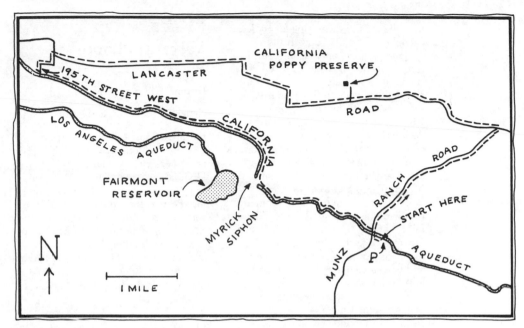

steady ascent to the aqueduct .6 mile ahead. Bikers turn southeast here onto the California Aqueduct Bikeway, which runs along the north levee of the aqueduct.

Hidden by the ridge directly south of the aqueduct is Los Angeles' major water source: the Los Angeles Owens River Aqueduct. Draining the watershed of the eastern Sierra, it supplies Los Angeles with 80 percent of its water. The two aqueducts run roughly parallel to one another, less than a half-mile apart, along this section of the Antelope Valley; and both of them are only four miles from the San Andreas Earthquake Fault. (*Note:* A short trip by car continuing south on Munz Ranch Road about 1 mile from the parking area leads to Elizabeth Lake, a sag pond created by

the San Andreas Fault, and allows views of the narrow valley also formed by the fault.)

Several bridges along the aqueduct provide a surreal touch. Each bridge rises over, not the aqueduct, but a second aqueduct riding piggyback in mid-air across the main channel. Built at the base of dry washes flowing out of the hills, these miniature airborne aqueducts prevent flash floods from contaminating the main aqueduct by carrying the flood water over it.

The aqueduct disappears into the Myrick Siphon (14.7), which carries the water across a narrow, deep canyon, while bikers follow a steep pitched road into the canyon and back up again. In another mile the trail passes an intermittently marshy area populated with hundreds of frogs who sing an endless cacophony of croaks and shrills.

Soon a bizarre apparition looms into sight: a medieval castle rises up beside the bank of a small pond in the hills below the aqueduct. Shea's Castle (16.8) was built by an Angeleno Irishman named John Shea who evidently hoped to bring a touch of the old country to the California desert. Copied from a photograph of a Dublin castle Shea saw in a magazine, the manse was begun in 1918 and took 10 years to build. Burros were used to haul in all the materials for construction. This huge, turreted edifice has walls like a fortress, more than ample to repel marauding coyotes and rattlesnakes, and is securely fenced off so a closer look is not possible.

Shea had an unhappy end, which may say something about building castles in the sand. He lost his money and the castle in the stock market crash of 1929, and a few months later his wife died. He put her ashes in a chamois bag, hung it around his neck and committed suicide by jumping off the Santa Monica Pier. This story is told in *A Guidebook to the Mojave Desert of California* by Russ Leadabrand (Los Angeles: Ward Ritchie, 1966). The book, now out-of-print, can be found in libraries and is an excellent guide to the area.

The trail soon returns to the parking lot off Munz Ranch Road (17.9), where the trip ends.

# RIDE 34

# Valyermo Loop

**Distance:** 18.8 miles round trip

**General Location:** Pearblossom

**Features:** The desert hills north of Pearblossom contain some of the area's most spectacular scenery, including the Devil's Punchbowl. This ride follows the aqueduct through these hills, drops into Pearblossom, then returns to the aqueduct via Valyermo Road, allowing a side trip to beautiful St. Andrew's Priory, a monastery sheltered in an isolated oasis in the hills. This route was laid out by Father Molaise, a monk at St. Andrew's who rides these hills daily.

**Difficulty:** Strenuous

**Elevation Gain:** 240 feet, Antelope Valley floor to the Fort Tejon Siphon

**Getting There:** Take the Golden State Freeway (I-5) 3.9 miles north from its intersection with the San Diego Freeway (I-405), then turn northeast onto the Antelope Valley Freeway (Highway 14). Drive 30 miles and turn east onto the Pearblossom Highway. Drive 4.4 miles to the Four Points intersection, which has a light. The Pearblossom Highway turns southeast here; follow it 11.4 miles, then turn south at 165th Street. Drive almost 2 miles and park at the California Aqueduct parking on the east side of the road. The parking area has a pit toilet but no picnic tables.

**Finding the Trail:** Cross 165th Street, lift bikes over the entrance barrier, and ride west on the aqueduct bikeway.

**Description:** The aqueduct runs 1.5 miles underground here through the Big Rock Siphon, which carries the water under the broad floodplain of the Big Rock Wash. The harsh desert landscape is interrupted by the incongruous emerald green lawns of the Crystalaire Country Club development south of the bikeway. North of the path cacti grow among boulders strewn about by ancient flash floods. The trail drops into the floodplain and soon crosses the swift flowing outlet of the wash and of Pallett Creek (1.6). The stream here is intermittent, depending on the rains; but when water does flow across the concrete bike path, bikers should slow down. The fast flowing water creates a big wake and soaks shoes and socks if riders attempt to speed through.

The trail soon climbs a steep hill to the top of the Big Rock Siphon (1.9), where it skirts the maintenance building and regains the north bank of the aqueduct. Crossing Valyermo Road at 2.2 miles, bikers will find a table under a shade ramada and a pit toilet.

The Valyermo rest stop marks the beginning of a 2-mile stretch of beautiful, wild desert country. The aqueduct here follows a contour line about 300 feet above the Antelope Valley, providing sweeping views of the valley and distant mountains.

The trail soon passes a grove of Joshua trees growing down the slope toward the valley floor. These bizarre, prickly trees, which once grew in forests in the Palmdale and Lancaster areas, are slowly being destroyed by development. They were named, so the story goes, by Mormon settlers traveling through the desert from San Bernardino to Utah. The trees reminded the Mormons of an Old Testament prophet pointing across the desert to the promised land, so they called them Joshua trees after the general noted for his knowledge of acoustics, who led the Israelites after the death of Moses. No one can tell how old these primordial trees are, for they grow no rings to mark their age. The Indians took the red and brown fibers from the inner bark of the Joshuas to weave into their baskets; and they ate the roasted flower heads. Development is already moving up this slope and will sooner or later demolish these magnificent desert sentinels. Growing near them along the trail are desert juniper.

On one trip through these Joshuas, I saw a coyote trotting across the hill. He stopped to check me out with his wild yellow eyes, decided I was an unwelcome intruder and loped off.

At the Longview Fishing Access (4.4), with toilets and water (faucet didn't work when I was there), the bikeway leaves the aqueduct and becomes a marked bike route along Fort Tejon Road. Leave the Longview parking lot, turn south on Longview and ride .4 mile. Turn west on Homer, a little used cutoff from Longview to Fort Tejon. It avoids a steep uphill climb at the end of Longview. Ride .2 mile on Homer, then turn west on Fort Tejon. After a fairly level ride along the shoulder of Fort Tejon for 3.5 miles, our ride leaves the bike route and turns north on 96th Street for an exhilarating downhill run to the valley floor at Pearblossom Highway (9.9).

The ride turns east along the highway, which has a broad shoulder marked by a white line, providing a safe lane for bikers. The trail returns to Longview (14.2), where bikers head south for .5 mile to the intersection with Valyermo Road. Turning east onto Valyermo, the trail begins a long, steady grade returning to the aqueduct (17.0).

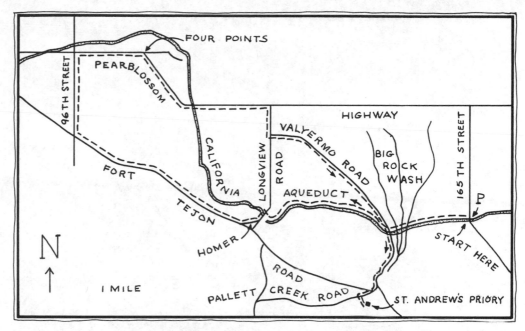

**Linking:** An additional 3.2 mile loop continuing up Valyermo Road leads bikers to St. Andrew's Priory. This beautiful monastic retreat, formerly the Hidden Springs Ranch, was acquired in 1956 by a community of Benedictine monks who had been in China. Fed by underground springs and shaded by groves of cottonwoods, the monastery is an oasis in the midst of the desert hills. The priory has rooms available for individuals and groups wishing to spend time in retreat. A gift shop sells ceramics made at the monastery, and an annual fall festival is held the last full weekend in September each year. For information, you may call the monastery 9 A.M. to noon and 1:30 to 5 Monday through Friday at (805) 944-2178.

To reach the monastery and visit its grounds or gift shop, continue riding south up Valyermo Road 1.3 miles to its intersection with Pallett Creek Road. Turn west on Pallett Creek, staying on the road as it passes an intersection with Fort Tejon Road. Follow signs to the monastery (1.6).

Returning to the aqueduct as it crosses Valyermo Road, bikers ride east on the aqueduct trail to the 165th Street parking lot (18.8).

A short sidetrip by car will lead bikers to the extraordinary rock formations in the Devil's Punchbowl County Park. Return to the Pearblossom Highway, turn west to Longview and drive south up Longview past Fort Tejon and Pallett Creek roads to signs pointing to the park. These striking rock formations were formed by earthquake faults in the area. Hiking trails lead through the park, but good views may be had from the visitor's parking lot.

# V   The Tough Ones

*Been Down so Long*
*It Looks Like Up to Me.*

—RICHARD FARINA

The rides in *L.A. Bike Rides* are designed to allow weekend bikers to get in condition gradually by progressing through easy, moderate and difficult trips. Once in shape, bikers will find themselves looking for more challenging workouts. The three rides described here require stamina, aerobic conditioning, sturdy leg muscles and a calloused posterior. They offer bird's-eye views of Greater Los Angeles and the far horizon of the Pacific, and one ride takes bikers from the San Gabriel Mountains to the Pacific Ocean and back.

Bikers who try these rides, like them and want more of the same may wish to join the Bicycling Section of the Sierra Club, (213) 387-4287, or the Los Angeles Wheelmen, (213) 533-1707. Both of these groups offer challenging bike rides.

The rides are:

**Ride 35.** The Big Loop. An 87 mile ride from the mountains to the ocean and back following three rivers.

**Ride 36.** Palos Verdes Peninsula: Up and Over. A 21 mile ride climbing steeply over the crest of the Palos Verdes Hills.

**Ride 37.** Mulholland Drive: the Spine of Los Angeles. A 16 mile ride along the crest of the Santa Monica Mountains.

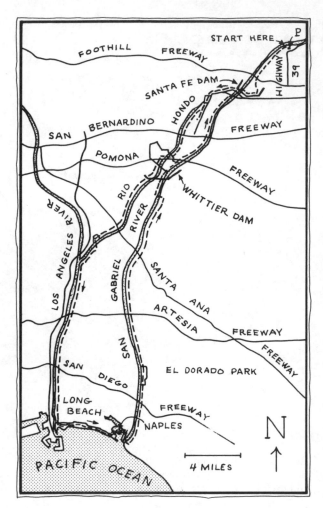

# RIDE 35

# The Big Loop

**Location:** Azusa, Irwindale, El Monte, South El Monte, Rosemead, Montebello, Downey, Bell Gardens, South Gate, Hollydale, Paramount, Long Beach, Seal Beach, Rossmoor, Lakewood, Cerritos, Norwalk, Santa Fe Springs, Los Nietos, Whittier, Pico Rivera, and Arcadia

**Distance:** 86.9 miles

**Features:** This trip follows three Angeleno rivers from the base of the San Bernardino Mountains to the Pacific Ocean and back. Although the ride is 87 miles, an incredible 75 of those miles are on contiguous bike trails totally separated from city streets. The ride begins where the San Gabriel River flows out of the mountains; it follows the San Gabriel to Santa Fe Dam, then utilizes a city road for a 4 mile ride to the headwaters of the Rio Hondo, which it follows to the Pacific Ocean. Crossing Long Beach by bike trail and 3.6 miles of city streets, it follows the San Gabriel back to the mountains.

The scenery along the way is spectacular: a mountain range, three rivers, four major creeks, two dams, 23 parks, and an ocean. It's a ride where images of pastoral splendor mingle with those of blighted factories, where free rivers are suddenly boxed in cement, oil wells pump in the middle of parks, cacti grow next to strawberry plants, and bag ladies share the bike path with long distance cyclers.

**Difficulty:** Strenuous

**Getting There:** From both the Foothill Freeway (I-210) and the San Bernardino Freeway (I-10), exit north on Azusa Avenue (Highway 39). Follow Azusa and continue north to its juncture with San Gabriel Road; drive another .8 mile and park in the lot of the National Forest Information Center on the right.

**Finding the Trail:** The bike trail begins on the west side of San Gabriel Canyon Road opposite to and slightly north of the ranger station.

**Description:** Detailed descriptions of this ride and attractions along the way may be found throughout this book. The number sequence of rides to consult is: 2, 7, 8, 9, 10, 29, 65, 4, 3, and 2 again.

The following instructions pinpoint locations where the trail is confusing and give detailed directions for those segments on city streets not covered in other sections of the book.

The trail follows the east bank of the San Gabriel, then enters the Santa Fe Dam Recreation Area and continues up the road leading to the top of the dam. Following the crest of the dam, it descends the dam face to Arrow Highway (7.8).

Here, rather than crossing the highway and continuing along the river, bikers should ride west on Arrow 2.3 miles to Peck Road, then pedal south on Peck 1.7 miles to the entrance of the Peck Road Water Conservation Park (11.8) at Rio Hondo Parkway. The entrance is on the west side of Peck. Wheel bikes across a stretch of dirt at the west end of the parking lot onto a service road running along the south edge of the lake. Ride west to the Upper Rio Hondo Trail.

Following the east bank of the Rio Hondo, the trail enters the Whittier Narrows Recreation Area (16.5). To connect with the Lario Trail, follow the peripheral road counter-clockwise around the park. Watch for the Bike Trail sign on the right to the Lario Trail. This sign marks the entrance to the second half of the Upper Rio Hondo trail, which passes through some interesting bottomland in the Narrows, crosses San Gabriel Boulevard, then climbs the back side of Whittier Narrows Dam (21.3).

For access to the Lario Trail, lift bikes across the low barrier at the south edge of the parking lot at the dam. Ride east along the top of the dam, then turn down the first road dropping across the face of the dam. It's difficult to get lost on the Lario Trail. The trail follows the west side of the river to John Anson Ford County Park, where it turns abruptly east on a footbridge crossing the river. Bikers who miss this turn will find themselves at a deadend at the railroad tracks .7 mile later. The trail then follows the river's east bank to the confluence of the Rio Hondo and the Los Angeles River (30.0).

The trail continues along the east bank of the Los Angeles River all the way to its outlet into the Pacific in Long Beach (42.1).

Getting through Long Beach can be confusing. Exit the river trail and ride south ¼ block until you see the Bike Trail sign indicating the path running east through the parking lot. The trail circles the large headquarters of the California State University and Colleges, then continues quayside through Shoreline Park. At the trail junction, riders should take the trail that crosses the bridge over the lagoon, then follow the trail east past the high pedestrian overcrossing and viewing tower. The trail seems to peter out at the tower, but continue on the road.

At Shoreline Village the trail crosses the street and enters a path beside an iron picket fence. At the next trail intersection, again turn east and continue to the harbor's eastern jetty. Turn north, cross the parking lot and ride up the steep exit road to the intersection of Shoreline and Ocean Boulevard. (Shoreline ends here and continues north as Alamitos Avenue. Follow Ocean east for 2.8 miles, keeping right on Ocean when Livingston Drive angles off to the northeast.

Since Ocean becomes a divided street, riders must make a U-turn at 54th and ride back 1 block to turn north onto Bay Shore Avenue, which encircles Alamitos Bay. Turn east on Second Street, crossing the bridge to the islands community of Naples. Leave Naples across a second bridge, turn right onto Marina Drive, then east on the bridge across the mouth of the San Gabriel River (49.0). The bike trail proceeds north up the east levee of the river. Entry is by a bike gate just across the bridge.

The return ride along the San Gabriel is clearly marked. In El Dorado Park (54.4) bikers must exit the bike path at Spring Street, ride under Spring through a tunnel, then return to the levee. A similar bypass is necessary at the north end of the park under Wardlow Road. At San Gabriel River Parkway, the trail crosses to the west levee, where it remains to Santa Fe Dam. Riding off the face of Whittier Dam (70.3), riders will encounter a trail intersection. The river trail continues northeast along the levee. At the base of Santa Fe Dam (79.1), cross Arrow Highway and ride up the face of the dam. From this point the ride retraces in reverse the first 7.8 miles of the trip.

# RIDE 36

# Palos Verdes Peninsula Loop

**Distance:** 21.2 miles round trip

**General Location:** Palos Verdes Estates, Rancho Palos Verdes, Portuguese Bend, Rolling Hills, and Rolling Hills Estates

**Features:** Specatacular views of the Palos Verdes coastline and the Pacific Ocean from an elevation of 940 feet atop the Palos Verdes Hills make this ride the most breathtaking in the book, in all ways. After passing Marineland and the Wayfarers Chapel, the route climbs Palos Verdes Drive East and makes a serpentine descent through the wealthy, isolated and gorgeously landscaped enclaves of Rolling Hills and Palos Verdes Estates.

**Difficulty:** Very Strenuous. Only four miles of this ride are on separate bike paths; local roads serve for the remainder of the trip. The rebuilt road across the perpetual landslide at Portuguese Bend is an extremely narrow two-lane street with no shoulder and bumpy pavement.

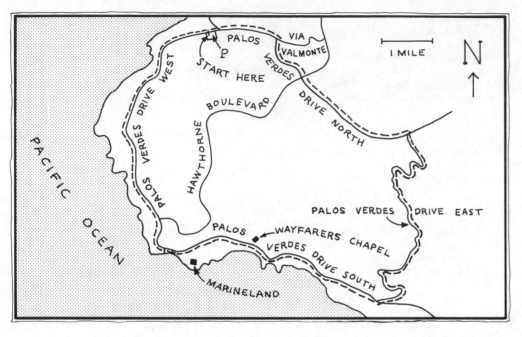

Point Vicente County Park (5.5). Bikers should fill water bottles here as there is no water for another 12 miles. This stopping point offers splendid views of the ocean, the rocky cove below and the Point Vicente lighthouse.

The road curves east at the park, and a separate bike path leads from Point Vicente past the Marineland entrance .5 mile ahead. Continuing east, bikers will soon see the Wayfarers Chapel. A stunning glass church designed by Lloyd Wright, the son of Frank Lloyd Wright, it sits north of Palos Verdes Drive South at 7.1 miles. The graceful, soaring structure is surrounded by beautifully landscaped grounds visible as cyclists continue east.

A sign at 7.5 miles warns bikers they are entering the Portuguese Bend land-slide area. Earth movement in the area has chewed up the road, which is now a narrow two-lane street without shoulders. It should be negotiated with extreme care by bikers; there is no margin for error. Water pipes through the Bend are laid on top of the ground because of the area's instability.

Santa Catalina Island looms on the horizon as the route turns east up Palos Verdes Drive East (9.8) and climbs a seemingly perpendicular grade through several hairpin curves to the highest elevation of the trip, 940 feet near the entrance to Marymount School. Pullouts on the way up offer resting spots and spectacular views looking back over the Pacific.

A freewheeling descent down the north slope of the hills past the Miraleste Delicatessen (13.2) takes riders to a separate bike path beginning at Conestoga Drive (15.8). Sheltered from the ocean winds, the north slopes

Because of the difficulties here, bikers are advised to take this ride early in the day before traffic builds up.

**Elevation Gain:** 780 feet, Palos Verdes Drive South near Point Vicente to the high point on Palos Verdes Drive East.

**Getting There:** From the San Diego Freeway (I-405), exit south on Hawthorne Boulevard. Drive 5.7 miles and turn west on Via Valmonte. At Palos Verdes Drive North turn north and follow the raod to its intersection with Palos Verdes Boulevard and Palos Verdes Drive West. Stay left onto Palos Verdes Drive West; then turn left almost immediately into parking at Malaga Cove Plaza. Parking is marked with 2- and 3-hour limits, not enforced on Sunday. Saturday and weekdays it is best to park on adjacent Street.

**Finding the Trail:** Ride to the west end of Malaga Cove Plaze, then ride west on Palos Verdes Drive West.

**Description:** The first segment of this ride follows the same route as the Palos Verdes Peninsula Coastline ride. (Ride 27) Leaving Malaga Cove Plaza, the route climbs the first grade, a gradual 2-mile ascent to an excellent view of Bluff Cove below. A slumped side road besides Palos Verdes Drive is the first evidence of the unstable ground conditions on the peninsula.

The road soon divides, passing through a pleasant residential area and past a shopping center (2.7). At Hawthorne Boulevard (4.7), the road dips to of these hills are thickly wooded with groves of eucalyptus. Horse trails abound, and bikers will often see horses and riders crossing the road. A sense of rural isolation pervades the scene, and it is difficult to remember that urban Los Angeles is less than five miles away.

Turning west on Palos Verdes Drive North (16.2), the trail leads to a grassy square at the intersection fo Rolling Hills Road (17.4). Benches, a water faucet and bike racks provide a pleasant rest stop. Passing Crenshaw Boulevard (18.0), the route returns to a separate bike path. At the major intersection of Palos Verdes Boulevard and Palos Verdes Drives North and West, bikers should stay left to Palos Verdes Drive West. The turn into Malaga Cove Plaza (21.2) is just past the intersection.

# RIDE 37

# Mulholland Drive: The Spine of Los Angeles

**Distance:** 16.2 miles round trip

**General Location:** Santa Monica Mountains

**Features:** This roller coaster ride along the crest of the Santa Monica Mountains offers exhilarating views of Los Angeles: north across the San Fernando Valley to the San Gabriel Mountains and south

across central Los Angeles to the Palos Verdes Hills and the great curve of the Pacific Ocean beyond.

On weekdays Mulholland Drive is used as an expressway for commuter traffic from the San Fernando Valley to Los Angeles. The two-lane road is narrow, most of it is without shoulders, and stretches of the pavement are rutted and bumpy. Why, one might ask, should anyone ride a bicycle here? Because the scenery is nothing short of spectacular, and on a clear day this bird's eye view of Los Angeles can't be matched. Early Saturday and Sunday mornings, Mulholland Drive is deserted, leaving bikers free to enjoy a ride on top of Los Angeles.

**Difficulty:** Strenuous

**Elevation Gain:** The entire road rolls along the spine of the Santa Monicas over a series of high points that gain around 100 feet, then drop. The single biggest gain is climbing out of Sepulveda Pass from the San Diego Freeway overpass to the end of the paved section of Mulholland, a slow, steady gain of 210 feet in 1.3 miles.

**Getting There:** Exit the Hollywood Freeway (Highway 101) west on Barham Boulevard to Cahuenga Boulevard, which parallels the west side of the freeway here. Drive south on Cahuenga. Jog right to Wilson Drive before the Mulholland overpass; continue south on Wilson and turn right onto Mulholland. Drive west on Mulholland past Laurel Canyon Boulevard and turn south almost immediately into Laurel Canyon Park.

Exit the Ventura Freeway (Highway 101) south on Laurel Canyon Boulevard. Drive about 3.6 miles and turn west on Mulholland Drive. Turn south almost immediately into Laurel Canyon Park.

**Finding the Trail:** Ride up the short, steep entry road from the parking lot at Laurel Canyon Park and ride west on Mulholland Drive.

**Description:** A steady climb of 140 feet from the park entrance to Allenwood Road (0.5) leads bikers to Vista Point, a small, dramatically landscaped viewing area north of Mulholland. Broad wooden stairs lead to a high point atop a rocky crest affording striking views across the San Fernando Valley. This small, beautifully situated park was purchased and developed by the Santa Monica Mountains Conservancy. Vista Point is one parcel of a thin corridor of land through the Santa Monicas acquired as part of the Santa Monica Mountains National Recreation Area. Vista Point has a water faucet and par course, should anyone need additional exercise.

Continuing west 1 mile (west is a relative term on this road since it continually twists and turns), bikers arrive at a second unnamed turnout on the right with several parking places. By climbing a short embankment beside the parking area, visitors are rewarded with one of the best views on the ride. The viewpoint is situated so bikers may see the entire San Fernando Valley cupped at the base of the San Gabriel Mountains.

Mulholland remains fairly level until Coldwater Canyon Park (2.5). This park is the home of the Tree People, the volunteer organization that has helped plant more than 500,000 new trees in Los Angeles. The group salvages bare

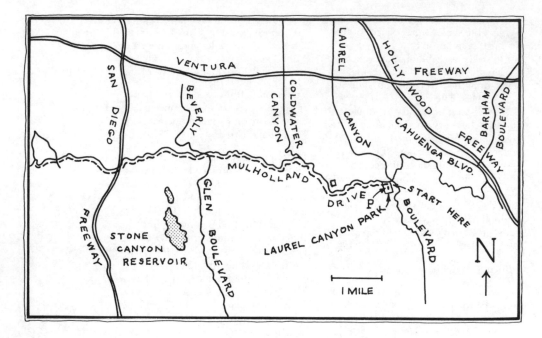

root trees unsold by nurseries and distributes them throughout the country in low income areas. They have replanted entire areas of the San Gabriels with smog resistant trees to replace the pines killed by smog. One-hour tours of Tree People headquarters and nature trails in Coldwater Canyon Park begin at 11 A.M. Sundays. Call (213) 769-2663 for information.

Cyclists follow a welcome downhill stretch on Mulholland after leaving the park. Near Java Drive (3.8) hills to the south fall away, and bikers have their first views of the distant Palos Verdes Peninsula and Pacific Ocean.

Sweeping views continue to Deep Canyon Drive, and the road widens as it approaches Benedict Canyon Drive (4.4) and Beverly Glen Boulevard (4.7). Small grassy areas at each of these cross streets provide pleasant resting areas.

Stone Canyon Reservoir is visible to the south as bikers approach the downhill run to Sepulveda Pass, where Mulholland crosses over the San Diego Freeway at 6.8 miles.

A steady, taxing uphill run .5 mile past Calneva Drive carries bikers to the high point on Mulholland (8.1), where the pavement and the ride end.

The return trip is by the same route in reverse.

# INDEX